INDEX

INDEX ON CENSORSHIP 4 2000

INDEX

Volume 29 No 4 July/August 2000 Issue 195

WEBSITE NEWS UPDATED WEEKLY
www.indexoncensorship.org
contact@indexoncensorship.org
tel: 020 7278 2313
fax: 020 7278 1878

Index on Censorship (ISSN 0306-4220) is published bi-monthly by a non-profit-making company: Writers & Scholars International Ltd, Lancaster House, 33 Islington High Street, London N1 9LH. *Index on Censorship* is associated with Writers & Scholars Educational Trust, registered charity number 325003
Periodicals postage: (US subscribers only) paid at Newark, New Jersey.
Postmaster: send US address changes to *Index on Censorship* c/o Mercury Airfreight International Ltd Inc, 365 Blair Road, Avenel, NJ 07001, USA
© This selection Writers & Scholars International Ltd, London 1999
© Contributors to this issue, except where otherwise indicated

---

Subscriptions (6 issues per annum)
Individuals: Britain £39, US $52, rest of world £45
Institutions: Britain £44, US $80, rest of world £50
Speak to Tony Callaghan on 020 7278 2313

EDITORIAL

Sporting lies

O ur worship of sport and our worship of big bucks have become a seamless unity. As athletes from all over the world head off to Australia (p115) for the Olympic Games, *Index* looks at the concentrations of wealth and power driving this now global industry, and the effects on players, spectators and communities. Who and what is being marginalised or extinguished? Mike Marqusee reflects that 'as media empires and sponsors increasingly seek control and even ownership of sporting institutions, the conquest and exploitation of markets threaten to ruin this delightfully trivial yet endlessly creative exercise of human faculties' (p38).

The money pouring in has changed the spectacle of sport and who watches it, raising its social status, leading to inflation in ticket prices, forcing fans with lower incomes out of live events and prime-time sport on TV. Money has also changed the nature of sport. As Gary Whannel says, 'We seem a long way from the days when sport was regarded as character building' (p48). There is cheating to win – Jim Firstle points out that the financial and political imperatives to win are now so great that it's hard for an ambitious athlete to resist the temptation of drugs (p65). And there is cheating to lose – as recent match-fixing revelations in cricket and football demonstrate. Meanwhile, sport acts more and more as a serious source of cultural reference and, more disturbingly, norms of behaviour, as the media transforms sports stars into role models they don't live up to.

And of course sport is highly politicised, used by politicians to sell values (p72) and by dissidents against repressive regimes (p77). Colin Tatz's revelations on the exclusion of Aborigines in Australia's sporting history – censored *in* as well as out (p130) – also reflects John Hoberman's concerns that sporting success may have created a post-colonial identity for black athletes in the US (p57). Whatever the story, sport seems to have been transformed into a 'public mania, manipulated for commercial and political advantage'.

In Australia, the media is close to an oligopoly, life expectancy for indigenous people is 20 years less than for non-indigenous, and the issue of free speech has a habit of turning into one of national identity. *Index's* file reveals a country often 'exuberantly inclusive' (p118) but also grappling with bigotries old and new. ❑

contents

A whirlwind of global capital has engulfed the sporting world. Gone are its lofty ideals and ethical concerns, replaced by a collusion of money and media

p36

Australia has seen more censorship laws passed in four years of John Howard's government than ever before in its history

p130

Russian arm wrestling: Putin 0 Gusinsky 1 – Special Report p25

5   EDITORIAL Ursula Owen
8   LETTERS

10   IN THE NEWS

     NEWS ANALYSIS
19   FIJI David Robie Melanesian dominoes
22   BRITAIN Julian Petley Video victories
25   RUSSIA Irena Maryniak Trial of strength
26   RUSSIA Elena Rykovtseva The awkward brigade
28   RUSSIA Yegor Yakovlev Endemic disease
29   RUSSIA Mikhail Gorbachev Citizens' watch
30   RUSSIA Sergei Kovalev Men and messiahs
31   RUSSIA Vitaly Tretyakov A lesson in spin

36   THIS SPORTING LIE
38   Mike Marqusee This sporting lie
48   Garry Whannel Stars in whose eyes?
55   Banned Sports
57   John Hoberman Behind the mask
62   Jon Entine Breaking the taboo
65   Jim Firstle Temptation
70   Fa'ezeh Hashemi Flying the chador
72   Simon Martin Modern Mussolinis
77   Simon Kuper Cheering the enemy
80   War by other means

84   FLASHPOINTS Syria
86   INDEX INDEX

114 AUSTRALIAN RULES
116 David Marr Suspect pleasure
118 Phillip Adams Wowsers on parade
126 Terry lane A SLAPP in time
130 Colin Tatz Uneven playing field
136 Margo Kingston Crime and punishment
138 Stolen generation
142 Chris Masters Behind the wire
146 Robbie Swan Sex, life and video
149 Jane Mills Two smacks & out!
153 Irene Graham Purity postponed
156 Christine Nicholls Cutting edge

     CULTURE
162 Diran Adebayo Batting collapse
166 CLR James Cricket in West Indian culture
172 Romaine Moreton The Silence of Blackness

174 BABEL A sporting chance
184 DIARY Grant Ferrett Till the next time
190 LETTER From Kigali

LETTERS

Ignorance and pettiness
From Christopher Hitchens, Washington DC

Earlier this year, I received a series of telephone calls and emails from an American reporter named Greg Palast, who was then working in London for the *Observer*. He told me a good deal that I already knew, including the fact that the Official Secrets Act was an enemy of free inquiry. He further informed me that Britain had no written constitution enshrining the rights of the citizen. And he asked me to sign a petition repudiating the police threat to proceed against the *Guardian* and the *Observer* in the matter of David Shayler. This I gladly did, or rather, this I did as a matter of course and a matter of principle.

Now, this same Greg Palast contributes a hastily written article to *Index on Censorship* 3/2000, entitled 'Kissing the Whip'. The article deals with those journalists and editors who found reasons *not* to defy D-Notices and other forms of harassment practised by the national security state. Its last sentences read: 'Britons, as they constantly remind me, are subjects not citizens. British-born journalist Christopher Hitchens, scourge of authorities on two continents, stunned Americans by submitting to deposition by US government prosecutors during the impeachment trial of President Bill Clinton. Clearly, habits of subjugation die hard.'

Everything in this passage is either false or irrelevant. The House Judiciary Committee, which prepared the case against Clinton, is not an arm of the US government. The White House and the presidency – this must be tolerably well known by now – *are* arms of the executive branch. I did not 'submit' to any process, but freely agreed to a request for my testimony. I testified against the government, in other words. I did so because I believe that President Clinton was guilty of gross abuses of power, and because I had some evidence with which to support said testimony. If Mr Palast does not understand the impeachment provisions of the United States Constitution, or even the elementary distinction between Congress and the state, he has no business patronising the hapless Brits for their lack of a Bill of Rights. And, if he believes me to be a whip-kisser, he has no business calling me at home and recruiting me to sign a petition that, through the agency of Anthony Barnett (I was an original signatory of Charter 88 in 1988), I had signed anyway.

What on earth is *Index* doing when it allows its space to be wasted, and its reputation for seriousness lowered, by ignorance and pettiness of this sort?

Religous intolerance
From Jeremy Teppig, Pennsylvania

I am alarmed that France is proposing to restrict religious freedom and the expression of religious ideas. In fact, Bills are in the making proposing prison sentences for the public expression and discussion of these religious ideas. [*'A Bill to reinforce the prevention and repression of cult groups'*, currently before the French Senate.] The ground is being prepared to stifle men and women who have strong beliefs. We must act now to prevent the

taking of prisoners of conscience, so as to not have to fight for their release after the fact.

Damning the stream
Huyu-Mwananchi, Nairobi

What's with all the streaming audio on your website? We in the South often rely on older PCs without speakers and behind government and employers' firewalls. It's no good putting articles on Internet censorship on Real Player audio; we cannot see and download it because of 'security' reasons. This is the most effective censorship of the net and you've fallen for it. Irony? Or something more sinister? Where are the text only versions for your worldwide readership?

ONE WORLD BROADCASTING AWARDS

At a dinner on 15 June, held to celebrate the annual One World Broadcasting Awards, *Index on Censorship* won the Magazines, Journals and Periodicals Award for their issue on Tribes, guest-edited by Hugh Brody and Ted Chamberlin. Jon Snow, who announced the awards, commented on the impressive entries in the section, all giving a voice to those in danger of having none, and singled out *Index* as 'a radical and valuable work which draws the reader into the reality of life as lived by indigenous peoples and examines their engagement with a world that considers them beyond modernity'.

Musket-shy A 25-foot-high ceramic mural of a musket-toting Harriet Tubman leading slaves to liberation on the Underground Railroad has upset the group that had planned to display it in Baltimore. Associated Black Charities Inc says the piece could be construed as 'racist and violent'. The group asked artist Mike Alewitz to replace the musket with a staff, but he refused. Tubman, a Maryland native, is the subject of five Alewitz murals to be installed throughout the state this summer.

Dog-ism Organisers of a rally opposing a ban on fighting dogs in Berlin cancelled plans to put yellow Stars of David on their pets as they paraded them through the city in May. Protestors had felt the yellow star would highlight the 'discrimination' suffered by their dogs. The Jewish community was appalled. Paul Speigel, president of the Central Council of Jews in Germany, said, 'This is repulsive tastelessness that insults every victim of the Holocaust.'

Delete function Kevin Mitnick cannot talk, write or have any other kind of contact with computers, cellphones or computer networks, concluded a judge in Los Angeles. Such activities violate a condition of his release from prison. Mitnick became a hackers' martyr after leading the FBI on a three-year manhunt that ended in 1995 when investigators traced his electronic footprints to an apartment in Raleigh, North Carolina. He is said to have cost companies and institutions millions of dollars by penetrating confidential computer systems.

● **Buon appetito** Florentines wanted to stop fictional flesh-eater Hannibal Lecter from consuming his victims in their backyard. The Greens and the Popular Party tried to prevent a particularly gruesome scene from the sequel to *Silence of the Lambs* being filmed in the Palazzo Vecchio, a Renaissance monument to good taste. They said the three-day shoot of *Hannibal* would colour the city's image for an entire generation of cinema-goers. But the authorisation had already been given, so attempts to divert Hannibal's appetites came too late.

● ***Baise* line** A censorship row is brewing in the office of new French Culture Minister Catherine Tasca over two sexually explicit films directed by women. The films by Catherine Breillat and Virginie Despentes have reignited an argument over the use of graphic sex in French cinema. Breillat's *Une Vraie Jeune Fille* (A Real Young Woman) was made 25 years ago and only received its first screening on 7 June due to its allegedly shocking content. Despentes' *Baise-Moi* (Fuck Me) was scheduled for screening on 28 June despite protests that the movie debases sex by using shock for its own sake. No change there, then.

● **Define live** The BBC won a High Court order in mid-June banning TalkSport from labelling its radio coverage of the Euro 2000 competition 'live'. Rights to broadcast the tournament were held by BBC Radio 5 Live and the Capital Radio group, but TalkSport, owned by former *Sun* editor Kelvin McKenzie, had been broadcasting what it claimed was live coverage from a studio in Amsterdam. This turned out to be reporters watching and commentating on TV coverage, over an amplified recording of match 'noise' for atmosphere. TalkSport reporters, miles from the stadium were, however, perfectly positioned to commentate on the highlights from the post-match violence in the square below.

● **Out with a bang** Spare a thought for Benetton's art director Oliviero Toscani, fired in late April when his 'Death Row' advertising campaign caused the US chain Sears Roebuck to cancel a US$41m contract. Toscani can take some comfort in the subsequent re-emergence of the death penalty as a political issue, but for Gary Graham all debate is now redundant. The Texas Death Row prisoner was dragged kicking to the executioner's needle in June – to the huge discomfort of presidential candidate George Bush, the current Texas governor.

● **Dangerous language** English echoed around the control tower at Charles de Gaulle airport in Paris during the first-ever attempt by the French to work in the *lingua franca* of all European airports. The experiment in May lasted a pitiful 15 days before infuriated pilots regained their right to *parler français*. The shift to English-only in the bilingual control tower was made because Air France believed one language would be safer than two. Unfortunately, home-grown pilots were outraged and the ensuing arguments (in French) proved more dangerous than the original system.

● **Pop goes pop** Advertisements for the soft drink Sprite, featuring the enormously popular Taiwanese singer, A-Mei, were pulled from mainland China's TV after her rendition of the Taiwanese national anthem at the inauguration of newly-elected President Chen Shui-bian on 20 May. The order to stop airing the ads was sent to Sprite's parent company, Coca-Cola China, five days later. The head of a cross-straits body in China later claimed the ads were stopped because of a copyright dispute over the jingle she had sung. He said he hoped people wouldn't make too much of the 'misunderstanding'.

● **Municipal disorder** The controversial governor of Tokyo, Shintaro Ishihara, drew condemnation when he told a garrison of troops on 12 April they should be ready to deal with rioting 'foreigners' – he used the pejorative – in the event of an earthquake. Several thousand Korean residents were massacred in the wake of the 1923 earthquake following rumours of looting. The South Korean government called his remark 'deplorable'. He caused further furore on 28 April when he said, 'Since the Soviet Empire went, China is the only empire left that still believes in expansionism – that is how the Communist Party is trying to hold on to power.' China had barely finished spluttering its condemnation when he was at it again on 24 May, saying that if China invaded an independent

Taiwan, President Jiang Zemin would become the 'Hitler of Asia'.

● **Sorry, Adolf** German historians are up in arms after the country's top literary award, the Konrad Adenauer Prize, was bestowed on Professor Ernst Nolte, who has sought to play down the monstrosity and scale of Nazi war crimes. Nolte became an academic pariah in the 1980s by suggesting that National Socialism was a distorted mirror image of Bolshevism and that Hilter was not 'absolutely evil'. Though no revisionist like David Irving (*Index* 3/2000), Nolte is nonetheless regarded as a Hitler apologist. He was praised by judges for 'opening up the debate on wartime Germany'.

● **My Mum** President Sapurmurat Niyazov has again bestowed his paternal attention on Turkmenistan's female population (*Index* 3/2000). On 7 June, he issued a decree renaming the country's only women's magazine, *Ovadan* (Beautiful), after his dear old mother. Henceforth, the magazine will be called *Gurbansoltan Edzhe*. But Turkmen women are used to name changes at the long-running magazine. It was called *Women of Soviet Turkmenistan* under Soviet rule and spent a while as *Hard Working Woman* after independence.

● **That's all, folks!** The hottest TV show in Cuba in recent months has been *Roundtable*, a talk show dedicated to the Elian Gonzalez case. The 2-3 hour extravaganza aired on both state-run channels daily at 5pm, often with President Fidel Castro conspicuously in the audience. The 'concept' was to run unedited clips from US news and current affairs programmes, featuring exiles in Miami and US politicians launching scathing attacks on Castro and his policies. The clips were then dissected by panellists as examples of the 'lies' fed to the US public. In another first, the show featured what for many Cubans was their first glimpse of the Internet – a medium banned on the island – as *Roundtable* showed viewers what was being written about the Elian case on the world's websites. Ironically, fellow students of the six-year-old national hero, who returned home on 29 June, had to suffer several months disruption to their preferred fare of undiluted cartoons normally shown in the 5pm slot.

● **Fly on the wall** CNN-
Turk's evening news on 31 May
showed scenes of torture filmed by
a secret camera at the Security
Directorate in Istanbul four years
ago. The footage showed Chief
Superintendent Suleyman Ulusoy,
aka 'Suleyman the Hose', beating
men and women detainees with a
length of rubber hose. Ulusoy is
notorious for having targeted
transvestites and street children in
the early 1990s. General Secretary
of Security Turan Genc, criticised
CNN-Turk for broadcasting the
scenes, claiming the programme
aimed to discredit the police at a
time. When journalists asked
Istanbul's security director, Hasan
Ozdemir, whether Ulusoy had
been suspended, he shouted,
'Should we suspend whoever you
want? You are trying to govern the
country!' Now an investigation has
been launched – against CNN-
Turk for showing the footage.

● **Sect crime** Legislation by
the French parliament in June
recognised the new criminal
offence of 'mental manipulation',
which it intends to punish with a
maximum fine of £50,000
(US$70,000) and five years
imprisonment. The law, which is
specifically aimed at 173
'dangerous' religious groups,
allows judges to order the
dissolution of any sect whose
members are convicted of a
criminal offence. It bans sects from
advertising, opening missions or
recruiting for new members near
schools, hospitals and retirement
homes. The legislation was
denounced as fascist by the
Church of Scientology, who were
supported by the Catholic Church.
It said the law would lead to
'judicial excess' and discriminate
against genuine religions.

● **BigBrother.com** As *Index*
goes to press, Britain's controversial
Regulation of Investigatory Powers
Bill is stalled in the House of
Lords. If the Labour government
manages to overcome the Lords'
opposition – which is backed by
business and human rights groups
– the Bill will become law in the
autumn. It will give the security
services new powers to intercept
emails and monitor data traffic. No
warrant will be required to
intercept communications data,
and all interceptions and
monitorings will be surrounded by
a permanent cloak of secrecy.
There is no legal way of learning
that emails have been intercepted.

Tim Berners-Lee, inventor of
the Web, said on 11 June that the
legislation would stifle the growth
of the Internet in Britain, and that
the Bill would have been thrown

out 'in a second' in the US.

Responding to reports from the Institute of Directors, the British Chamber of Commerce and others, the government has introduced amendments to compensate industry for direct expenses and to inform the directors of Internet Service Providers of taps made to their equipment, but many human rights concerns remain unaddressed.

● **It's a book, dummy** The publication of Haidar Haidar's book *A Banquet for Seaweed* by Egypt's Ministry of Culture revived the long-simmering tension between conservatives and liberals that had surfaced in the Nasr Abu Zaid case in the 1990s (*Index* 4/1996 et al).

Within a month, the newspapers *Al Shahab* and *Osaba* had published selected extracts they claimed depicted the prophet Mohammed as a 'skirt-chaser'. Minister for culture, Farouk Hosni, quickly knuckled under in the face of protest, and ordered all copies to be withdrawn from bookstores. This was too little too late for *Al Shahab*, chief organ of the Labour Party. On 4 May, it organised a meeting to denounce Haidar and Hosni, attracting a number of scholars from Al-Azhar

University. On 7 May, Al-Azhar's dean, Ahmed Omar Hashem, denounced the novel in a letter to the state-owned *Al Akhbar*, which, in turn, provoked an anti-Haidar protest by Al-Azhar students in which 50 were injured. None of the students interviewed by local media confessed to having read the book, though a few conceded that the rally was a God-given opportunity to protest Egypt's parlous economic conditions.

On 9 May, the People's Assembly religious committee judged the book blasphemous and recommended burning it. The Ministry for Culture parried with its own committee, which found, unsurprisingly, that *A Banquet for Seaweed*, first published in Beirut in 1983, in no way insulted God or religion. But even as the committee spoke, officials from the prosecutor's office were hammering on the doors of Ibrahim Aslan and Hamdi Abu Galil, hapless editors at the Ministry for Culture's publication programme, with warrants for their arrest for 'belittling religion'. On 17 May, Al-Azhar's Sheikh Mohaamad Sayyed Tantawi put his oar in, saying the novel 'incites unrest and shakes the cohesion of national unity'. ❏

Arif Azad

MICHAEL GRIFFIN

Three cheers for the third estate

On 30 June, Sri Lanka's Supreme Court forced President Chandrika Kumaratunga to back down on the state of emergency legislation that imposed prior censorship on the media and put journalists at risk

The Supreme Court of Sri Lanka has ruled that the government acted illegally in closing down newspapers after its armed forces suffered a major setback in the Jaffna peninsula in the 17-year war against the secessionist Tamil Tigers in April.

The legislation on 3 May gave law enforcement authorities powers to arrest journalists, seize their property, block distribution and shut down newspapers under the broadly-defined grounds of 'national security'. Local journalists have been subject to a censorship regime since June 1998, but it was enforced only sporadically. The new regulations forced foreign correspondents to submit reports to the censor and blocked access to the BBC's Tamil and Sinhala services, the only impartial source of news for most Sri Lankans.

The authorities used the legislation on 19 May to close down the offices of the Tamil-language *Uthayan*, the only functioning newspaper in Jaffna, on the grounds that it was 'acting maliciously and detrimentally in publishing information that is biased towards the Liberation Tigers of Tamil Eelam (LTTE)'. The editor, N Vidyatharan, argued that because the civil war had disrupted telecommunications, he was unable to submit copy to Colombo for clearance. He urged the government to appoint a local censor.

Three days later, police occupied the printers of the weekly *Sunday Leader* in a bid to prevent publication of a front-page lampoon of the new information status quo, entitled 'War in Fantasyland'. The *Leader*, which has built up a reputation for criticising the privatisation of the national airline, the handling of the civil war and corruption in the procurement of military equipment, was banned for six months. The closure also disrupted production of the Sinhala-language *Irida Peramuna*, and five other titles in the Leader Group.

The three-judge panel delivered its unanimous verdict on 30 June in response to a petition from the Leader Group challenging the decision. The court ruled that because the chief censor's appointment had not been submitted to parliament for review within seven days, as required by law, the decision to close down the *Leader* was 'a nullity, and of no force or avail in law'. The judges ordered the government to pay the Leader Group 100,000 rupees (US$1,300) in court costs.

The *Sunday Leader* was one of ten newspapers to legally question the new rules, arguing that the 'Competent Authority' - the government's epithet for chief censor - was arbitrarily banning statements, articles and cartoons that did not contain any material prejudicial to national security or public order. 'There are no guidelines,' lamented Lalith Allahkone, editor of the *Daily Mirror*. 'There is nothing systematic on what they censor and what they don't censor.' By way of example, the litigants had cited an open letter of condemnation by the Sri Lankan Editors' Guild, that was scissored by the Competent Authority when submitted for approval by four independent newspapers, but published in full by papers in the state-owned Lake Group.

Sunday Leader editor Lasantha Wickrematunge played upon the inconsistencies of the censorship regime like an out-of-tune xylophone. 'For example,' he said, 'the newspaper was sent to the censor and then published spurious identical articles which clearly showed that the articles blaming the [opposition] United National Party (UNP) for the present state of the country were approved by the censor, while identical articles, replacing the UNP with the government, were censored *in toto*.' The *Leader* submitted a copy of a cartoon which had appeared in the state-controlled *Daily News* the week before, featuring the opposition leader Ranil Wickremasinghe. It then substituted the opposition leader's figure with that of President Kumaratunga. The first was approved, the other censored fully.

Curiously, ministers were quick to distance themselves from President Chandrika Kumaratunga's imposition of censorship until 21 August, when parliament is due to be dissolved in preparation for a new electoral campaign. 'Censorship has polarised an already polarised situation,' said media minister Mangala Samaraweera, while foreign minister Lakshman Kadirgemar considered censorship 'really counter-productive'. 'I can see for myself it is being applied in a very heavy-handed way.' He said he had urged President Kumaratunga to consider easing the restrictions, but Kumaratunga - whose mother, former President Sirimavo Bandaranaika, imposed a similarly harsh censorship regime from 1970 to 1977 - told the Indian daily, *The Hindu*, on 23 May: 'Ha! You call them newspapers. I call them filth-mongering newsheets. This is not a normal democratic situation.'

Indeed, it is not. The loss of Elephant Pass, a strategically crucial base to the south of Jaffna, by government forces in April this year has opened not only the road to victory to the Tigers, but a rare opportunity for the press to probe the management of a war that, officially, costs Sri Lanka US$850m a year. Opportunities for corruption are enormous, as the *Leader's* Wickrematunge pointed out. 'We published extracts from the files of the air force, that they had bungled and bought in equipment that was not working. If Sri Lanka's integrity and sovereignty is endangered by the LTTE, it is also endangered by the government itself. We have taken the position that the government and the opposition should get together and negotiate with the LTTE. A large body of Sri Lankans want peace and, as long as it falls short of a separate state, they will accept it.' ❏

Michael Griffin

DAVID ROBIE

Melanesian dominoes

Two island nations in the Pacific are in the grip of coups by indigenous groups. Who's next?

The government of kidnapped Prime Minister Mahendra Chaudhry, Fiji's only Indo-Fijian prime minister in 30 years of independence, had achieved a modest economic succeeded in its first year in office. Indo-Fijians make up 44% of the islands' 800,000 population.

But on Friday 19 May, failed businessman and *kailoma* (part-Fijian) George Speight, along with renegade soldiers from the elite Counter Revolutionary Warfare unit, stormed parliament and took the Chaudhry government hostage in the name of 'indigenous Fijian paramountcy'. 'We're not going to apologise to anybody and we're not going to step back, and we're not going to be daunted by accusations of racism, or one-sidedness,' Speight declared. 'At the end of the day, it is about the supreme rights of our indigenous people in Fiji, the desire that it be returned – wholesome and preserved for the future.'

Many of Speight's group, like their leader, had dubious reputations: only five days before the coup, Speight appeared in Suva's High Court on charges of extortion. He had a grievance against Chaudhry's government for his dismissal as chief executive from Hardwood Corporation, Fiji Pine. Hardwood stood to lose lucrative timber deals were Chaudhry to remain in office.

However, Speight achieved his aims, without releasing his key hostages: abrogation of the 1997 multiracial constitution written after the coup of 1987; the resignation of Fiji's president, 80-year-old Ratu Sir Kamisese Mara; a non-elected indigenous administration; and an amnesty for the kidnappers, who risked the death penalty. Meanwhile, the country was descending into chaos: one month into the coup, some

4,500 people had lost their jobs after tourism collapsed, thousands more had their pay packets slashed, local schools closed, Fiji was partially suspended from the Commonwealth and EU aid was in doubt.

Fiji is not the only Pacific country in crisis. In the Solomon Islands, the people of Guadalcanal are attempting to push immigrant Malaitans off their island, a campaign that has forced an estimated 20,000 people – almost a quarter of the Malaitan population – to flee. The conflict is spearheaded by the Guadalcanal Revolutionary Army and the Isatabu Freedom Movement against various Malaitan groups. Both sides have carved out a small-scale but effective campaign of terror which has killed more than 60 people and stirred riots in the capital, Honiara. Like Indians in Fiji, the Malaitans are the most successful group in the Solomon Islands and this stirs resentment. Ousted Prime Minister Bartholomew Ulufa'alu, the target of the coup, is a Malaitan.

'The idea that coups d'état could spread like a virus in the Pacific should be taken seriously,' says *Samoa Observer* editor Savea Sano Malifa (*Index* 6/1998 *et al*). 'From Fiji to the Solomons, political uprising is now feared to be spilling over into Papua New Guinea and possibly Vanuatu.' Preoccupied with resolving a decade of secessionist war on the copper-rich island of Bougainville, Papua New Guinea has preferred to keep a low-key approach to troubles in other Pacific states. But one former prime minister, Sir Julius Chan, warns against such a casual attitude: 'We seem to have applied the Melanesian approach. You sit back, chew betel nut, look into the sky and wait to see what happens.'

Chan was forced out of office over the aborted Sandline affair in 1997, when South African-led mercenaries were recruited for an operation against the Bougainville Revoutionary Army rebels. As prime minister in 1980, Chan had responded to a call from the late Vanuatu leader, Father Walter Lini, to quell a rebellion on the island of Espiritu Santo. Ever since, he has been an advocate for a regional peacekeeping force with Papua New Guinea playing a pivotal role. As the Solomon Islands careered towards civil war and Fijians haggled over power, however, many questioned the future of the South Pacific Forum and the Melanesian Spearhead Group over their failure to broker peace deals in either country.

For some Pacific leaders, democracy is a seen as a 'foreign flower' that hasn't transplanted well; others argue that democratic constitutions are ill-suited to cope with the problems of national unity and intercommunal rivalry. Demagogues in Fiji have long 'whipped up the chimera of Indian dominance' to fan the fears of cultural insecurity. But Father David Arms, a Catholic priest and constitutional authority for the Fiji Citizens' Constitutional Forum, believes the Fijian constitution was a progressive document which safeguarded rights for the 51% indigenous population which has 57% overall control of both houses of parliament.

Others say this is not the real issue: the Pacific's political crises are more complex than straightforward ethnic conflict. Professor Yash Ghai of the University of Hong Kong, who had a hand in drafting the abrogated Fijian constitution, said: 'The troubles have been triggered by different factors in each of the states: in Papua New Guinea by the ravages of the Panguna mine; in Fiji by the orchestration of indigenous indignation against a government led by an Indo-Fijian; in the Solomon Islands by economic competition between resident and migrant communities.' The root of all three conflicts, he says, is in the pace of economic and technological change that has disrupted traditional values and structures, destabilised societies and reduced their economic and political self-sufficiency. The capacity, or even willingness, of Pacific governments to deal with these problems has steadily declined. ❏

David Robie, a New Zealand journalist, is the author of a book about the 1987 coups, Blood on their Banner: Nationalist Struggles in the South Pacific *(Zed, London 1989) and has a forthcoming book about Pacific media*

JULIAN PETLEY

Video victories

An appeal against UK censorship of 'porn' videos shed light on the mechanics of censorship and the role of the Home Office

According to a more than usually enraged *Daily Mail* on 17 May, 'a High Court judge yesterday gave the go-ahead for hardcore porn films to be sold legally in Britain'. The small but salient fact that you won't find them in any video outlet was drowned by the accompanying bile, but there lurks at the heart of this much-misreported story a significant victory over censorship of a ludicrous variety.

The story begins in 1996, when the director of the British Board of Film Classification (BBFC), James Ferman, was asked by Tom Sackville, parliamentary under-secretary of state for the Home Office, if the BBFC could liberalise the guidelines of the R18 category, which designates which videos may be sold only to over-18s in licensed sex shops. Why? Because the Metropolitan Police were concerned at the growth of black-market sex shops which took advantage of the fact that their legal counterparts could sell only tame material. Ferman was happy to agree.

The videos passed as a result of the new dispensation were still far less explicit than the conventional, hardcore porn videos legally available elsewhere in Europe – not to mention publications like *Rustler* now to be found on many newsagents' top shelves. When Jack Straw became home secretary and discovered what the BBFC was doing, he exploded, releasing to the press a letter criticising Ferman 'in the strongest possible terms' for his 'unacceptable, unilateral decision to liberalise the law'. He insisted the BBFC reverse its 'liberalisation' policy and let it be known that he was reviewing Ferman's position. In December 1997, he vetoed the appointment of Lord Birkett, the BBFC vice-president and a supporter of the liberalisation policy, as the board's new president. Having made his point, Straw then stepped out of the limelight and left the BBFC to deal with the consequences.

Straw's grounds for forcing the BBFC to reverse its policy hinged on his insistence that material passed during the 'liberal' period was of a 'strength' similar to material seized as obscene by Customs, or subject to forfeiture under Section 3 of the Obscene Publications Act (OPA). This ignored the fact that far stronger material has been regularly let off the hook by juries when defendants have elected to be tried by jury under Section 2 of the OPA – a right, incidentally, which they will no longer enjoy if Straw's plans to curb jury trials become law. Faced with this awkward fact, the Home Office changed tack, arguing that the R18s passed by the BBFC in the 'liberal' period would 'harm' any children who might view them and would thus fall foul of the Video Recordings Act – seemingly unaware that this undermined the very principle of classification-by-age-range on which the Act is founded, as well as the 'adults only' principle governing admission to licensed sex shops.

Meanwhile, distributors Sheptonhurst and Prime Time, which had relatively 'strong' material passed by the board during the 'liberal' period, now found that, with the old guidelines reinstated, the BBFC was refusing to pass similar material. Arguing that the BBFC had been inconsistent in changing its guidelines – and that it should anyway have consulted them before doing so – the distributors took eight of the board's refusals to the Video Appeals Committee.

'The board's decision to backtrack on liberalising the guidelines was completely irrational, since by this point there were already half a million copies of the "stronger" videos in circulation anyway,' said Greg Hurlstone of Prime Time. 'If they were really that concerned, they would have had to argue that these should be withdrawn. But, let's be honest, none of this was up to them anyway. These decisions were political and have been taken elsewhere all along'.

The appeal was heard in July 1999 and the distributors won, the majority of the committee concluding that the videos were 'suitable for sale uncut solely to adults in sex shops, and that the risk of any so sold being viewed by and causing harm to children or young persons is, on present evidence, insignificant'. The BBFC then applied for judicial review of the appeals procedure but, in May, this was dismissed by Mr Justice Hooper. Hence the *Mail*'s fury.

It was not alone. A raging Straw suddenly reappeared centre stage. Labour worthies Lord Bassam and Robin Corbett were propelled onto television to condemn the decision and the Home Office issued a statement to the effect that 'the home secretary believes that the situation is unsatisfactory and will be considering carefully whether there are any additional steps that can be taken to protect children from exposure to this sexually explicit material. Any such changes may require legislation.' A *Times* headline confidently asserted 'Porn law to be tighter after censors' defeat'.

In spite of the best efforts of the press, all Straw has actually announced is a consultation process. What appears to have happened is that the saner counsel of Home Office civil servants, who had supported the original 'liberalisation' of the R18 guidelines and were aghast at Straw's various interventions, has finally prevailed. The story isn't over until the consultation is concluded, of course, but it does demonstrate what can be achieved when distributors seriously challenge the censorship system – as opposed to conniving with it as major companies do. 'Right from the start,' explained Hurlstone, 'we were prepared to take it to Europe if we had to, and we always knew we would win.'

One should not overestimate the extent of the victory: the effective return of 'liberalised' guidelines permits only the blandest 'vanilla' porn on video, and still leaves the licensed sex shops at a considerable disadvantage compared to their illegal counterparts. Hurlstone concludes: 'Local councils should be instructed to license far more sex shops, selling the kind of hardcore porn you find elsewhere in Europe. The ultimate goal has to be parity with other European countries, which we'll certainly be pushing for and which, I reckon, will take another five years. Of course, this is a very sensitive issue politically, as we've all too clearly seen, but it's worth pointing out that porn is a multimillion pound industry which everywhere else raises a fortune in taxes. Think of all the hospitals you could build with the revenue from legalising it!'

A point neatly backed up, in fact, by a story in *The Times* on the very same day that it reported the judicial review in such disparaging terms. It concerned the Hot d'Or 2000 festival in Cannes, which revealed that porn films grossed £20bn (US$29.6bn) a year worldwide and that a former mortgage adviser from Northampton turned porn star was now earning £250,000 a year. Needless to say, this was not in Northampton, nor anywhere else in the UK. ❑

Julian Petley *is a lecturer in media and communication studies at Brunel University*

Trial of strength

O n 11 May, several dozen masked, armed police took over the Moscow offices of the media-banking consortium MOST in a raid which, the Federal Security Service (FSB) said, was to find evidence of tax irregularities and unauthorised eavesdropping. It raised instant fears of a more general clampdown on media freedom; Obshchaya gazeta published an issue devoted to the threats to the media and enlisted concerned individuals to voice their alarm at the possibility of worse yet. Then, a month later on 13 June, came the arrest of media tycoon Vladimir Gusinsky himself. Three days later, after widespread international protest, he was free: first round to Gusinsky and a rout for government forces, says the editorialist in Nezavisimayaa gazeta, warning that this is not the end of the matter.

As head of MOST, Gusinsky represents two of the most powerful sectors in Russia today – banking and the media. MOST controls the most influential nationwide private television network, NTV, as well as radio Ekho Moskvy, the daily Segodnya the weekly magazine Itogi. It also has a stake in Obshchaya gazeta and Novaya gazeta, and subsidises the St Petersburg daily Smena. The group has been critical of alleged corruption and intrigue in the Kremlin and, particularly, of the state's conduct of the war in Chechnya. MOST editors say Gusinsky's arrest had been threatened for months.

Gusinsky remains charged with embezzling US$10m of state funds; given the generalised culture of corruption and tax chaos, few companies can be certain of being entirely clean. The raid and Gusinsky's detention suggest a developing policy to rein in voices of opposition under the cloak of law enforcement; intimidate other groups critical of government; and curb the influence of an oligarch with a particular agenda and overtly western leanings. In a two-hour programme on prime-time TV on 20 June, Gusinsky warned of a return to Soviet-style political repression and declared that his arrest had been ordered personally by President Vladimir Putin. ❑

Irena Maryniak

ELENA RYKOVTSEVA

The awkward brigade

Some people pretend, and some even genuinely believe, there is no
threat to a free press in free Russia. Journalists are writing copy,
newspapers are being printed, broadcasting companies are broadcasting.
Look: no handcuffs, no one in jail, no labour camps! OK, so maybe they
tried to incarcerate that Alexander Khinshtein from *Moskovskii
Komsomolets* in a lunatic asylum: well, he shouldn't have been messing
around with forged documents, should he? OK, they let the Chechen
rebels seize Babitsky from Radio Liberty – serve him right. What was he
doing in enemy territory anyway? You can't generalise from a few
individual cases; and as far as a few organisations, newspapers, television
companies or whatever are concerned – well, there's absolutely nothing
to get upset about.

The Television Centre (TVC) is kicking up a fuss because the
government want to take away the Mayor of Moscow's frequency. Well,
that is all perfectly logical, too, and perfectly legal. The licence is
expiring, so he can fight for the frequency in open competition.

Everything in the garden is lovely. It may be annoying, but it's the
purest coincidence that a couple of awkward, wrong-headed journalists
fell foul of the law. It's equally coincidental that the television companies
that have fallen foul of financial, criminal and competition sanctions,
Independent Television (NTV) and TVC, are the only stations that
obstinately refuse to give air time to the government's apologists. The
chronology of these sanctions is also purest coincidence: NTV criticises
Voloshin, head of the presidential administration, and
Vneshekonombank demands early repayment of a multimillion rouble
credit. NTV declines to share the state's approach to reporting of the war
in Chechnya, and its shareholder Gazprom suddenly wants its money

back. NTV continues to view the newly elected president sceptically, indeed somewhat askance, and the president's bully boys pick a fight with Media-MOST's security.

Or are there, perhaps, just too many coincidences for us not to start generalising. The authorities don't simply dislike an awkward press, they want to get rid of it. The authorities are out to choke it materially and discredit it morally. The saga of Media-MOST's security service dealt a severe blow to the reputation of NTV. What did this story leave in the mind of Mr Average watching the state TV channels? That Gusinsky, the owner of NTV, is an agent of the CIA and Mossad, who spies not only on other companies' journalists, but on his own as well. Not only that, but NTV journalists make use in their investigations of materials obtained by the Gusinsky network's spying and bugging.

TVC can get in a flap, appeal to the public, and inform its viewers that both the legal censures it received have been annulled in arbitration, and that the competition is being run on an illegal basis, but the mechanism is already in motion, and the Ministry of the Press has no intention of cancelling the competition. It will go ahead quietly, behind closed doors, in a narrow circle of bureaucrats with a trio of lay representatives thrown in for appearances' sake, and with all the participants in the process under an obligation not to make public the creative conceptions of the bidders. 'Public opinion' has in any case already been softened up by the state broadcasting channels. Why should that thief, murderer, etc, Mayor Luzhkov, have a channel of his own anyway? There are better people with a claim to that frequency.

The major distinguishing feature of the present war against the awkward press is the participation in the aggression of those organs of the press which are totally compliant. The authorities, having opened a main front using the Federal Security Bureau, the Ministry of the Interior, the State Prosecution Service and the Ministry of the Press, have also opened a second front where the mass media owned by the state or controlled by Berezovsky batter their colleagues no less furiously. Luckily for President Putin, Berezovsky has long been a sworn enemy both of business magnate Gusinsky and of Mayor Luzhkov.

On this front, the state-owned Russian Radio and Television (RTR) and Berezovsky's All-Russian Television (ORT), there is no room for information emanating from their opponents. Nothing is heard of announcements from TVC about the lawless shenanigans of the Ministry of the Press or of protests by Media–MOST about illegal actions by government agencies, or about libels spread by the Federal Security Bureau, which showed on air a bugging device and 'spy data' which in fact had never been seized from Media–MOST.

TVC has gone to court and won; NTV is also suing the FSB, ORT, and RTR for libel and may well also win. However, the court victories of TVC have remained without consequences, and any 'victories' won by NTV are unlikely to be more helpful. The president promised to be rigorous, and if he were suddenly to leave the oppositional press in peace he would be breaking that promise: we can rely on him to fight on to the bitter end. Whose end that will be – the end of our democratically elected president or of those sections of the press he finds awkward – is still far from clear. ❏

Elena Rykovtseva *is a journalist with* Obshchaya gazeta
Translated by Arch Tait

YEGOR YAKOVLEV

Endemic disease

We Russians have suffered from an endemic disease that has raged for centuries; our faith in the good master, the good tsar or the good reformer is as strong now as it was in antiquity. Even now, after the outrageous raid on Media–MOST, many of my colleagues are particularly worried about just one thing: did the president know? If he did then, well then, that's really bad: but if he didn't, then all's not yet lost and there's hope yet.

It's all the same to me, frankly, whether this brutal raid happened with Putin's blessing or not. On the day Vladimir Vladimirovich [Putin] walked in triumphant isolation down that carpeted path across the

Kremlin to the throne, it became obvious that there was no point wasting any effort on trying to unravel the real state of affairs in Russian politics, its web of intrigue. We don't need conjecture, we need facts. And we have more than enough: from the Babitsky affair to the raid on Media–MOST; from the brief anti-terrorist operation that became an unending partisan war; to the ministry of truth that feeds on media repression. There have been enough calls to bring out the 'black box' that will reveal all, but it's simpler to read the one available book: Putin on Putin. *In the first person* makes it abundantly clear how incompatible Vladimir Vladimirovich's interpretation of the events of recent years is with, say, mine or that of my colleagues and friends. If the fall of the Berlin Wall, the unification of Germany, the purge of the KGB after the *putsch* were to us evidence of not having lived our lives in vain, these events awoke rather different feelings in Putin. And these were inspired not by temperament but by professional training and inclination. Addressing an audience that he is familiar with, Vladimir Vladimorovich observed that the group of FSB [former KGB] employees designated to work in government had handled their job just fine. The degree of truth in this little joke lends it a significance that is very far from funny. ❏

Yegor Yakovlev is the editor of Obshchaya gazeta

MIKHAIL GORBACHEV

Citizens' watch

I was very disturbed by the Media–MOST story; it smacks of provocation. I'm reminded of the raid on the Gorbachev Foundation in 1992. We were also blockaded by masked men, and people were handcuffed. Yeltsin said at the time that Gorbachev was taking too much on himself. Today, I have the feeling that someone has decided that the

Russian press is taking too much on itself. But the media, by definition, cannot take on too much. Without a free press people don't have a voice. They can be used as the authorities see fit; they can be manipulated.

Did the voters choose to be ruled by masked men in the March election? I find it hard to believe that raids like these can take place with the president's knowledge. If, indeed, it is with his knowledge, I personally feel very disappointed.

Did the organisers of the operation against Media–MOST realise what kind of response it would provoke in Russia and abroad? Or perhaps all this was planned because there is no serious economic and political programme: no serious steps have been outlined to take the country forward. So they've decided to make scapegoats out of the journalistic profession.

I'm also worried and dispirited by the apathy of the public. The journalists are having to defend themselves on their own. It's time we understood we shall never be a democratic state until we have learned to be citizens. ❏

Mikhail Gorbachev is former head of the USSR and now runs the Gorbachev Foundation in Moscow

SERGEI KOVALEV

Men and messiahs

I never expected such a crude, thuggish demonstration of strength, such an overt attempt to intimidate people. But at the same time, I'm convinced there will be no return to direct censorship. The most effective censors are still in our own heads. That is what the people who organise these masked attacks count on.

I'm quite sure the operation was sanctioned from the top. It would be absurd to assume that Putin was not aware of it. Remember the scandal in the Duma when *Yedinstvo* [a political grouping close to the government] made an alliance with the Communists? It seemed at the time as though Vladimir Vladimirovich knew nothing about it. It was terrifying to think that a faction whose leaders couldn't say a word without consultation with the Kremlin was suddenly, boldly in step with the Communists. What courage!

Today, it's just as hard to believe in this 'independence' as it is to be persuaded that the raid on Media-MOST was the work of an official from the procurator's office. But sadly, we are all complicit. We allowed ourselve to have these elections. And who but we should learn the lesson. People – especially people with a messianic tradition – can be wrong. The Germans have managed to acknowledge the errors they made in the twentieth century. Why do we still refuse to learn from our mistakes? ❑

Sergei Kovalev was the first human rights commissioner appointed by Boris Yeltsin but was later dismissed

VITALY TRETYAKOV

A lesson in spin

The attack on Media-MOST became something more – or less – than an attack on media freedom: it was an attempt to silence the most powerful independent voice in the country – and one with political ambitions?

Vladimir Gusinsky's brief but epic sojourn in prison shed instant light on the political psychology of Russian society today. All its hidden nooks and crannies suddenly were suddenly thrust into the spotlight. Since, according to some participants in the incident, the authorities took up arms against democratic freedoms and subsequently lost at least the initial phase of the campaign, it would be no bad thing to consider the lessons to be learned.

The second phase of the conflict is still ahead: neither the 'insurgents' nor those who resisted them have been crushed. Looking at it from the other side, however, it was MOST, with Gusinsky at its head, that took up arms against the Kremlin, and the Kremlin who responded with a none too successful counter-attack. So there can be no respite: things have only just begun.

But why did they release Gusinsky? At the very least, this represents a defeat for the authorities in an important battle, if not in the war as a whole. And after a fight that persisted for three whole days.

There are three main reasons that led to the retreat of the authorities. First, their actions had no support from any signficant social or political force. Second, the authorities understood that oligarch Gusinsky's public image was, with the help of a little public relations, swiftly turning into that of a leading dissident, a kind of Sakharov 2000. They must have calculated that his image could just as quickly be turned in the opposite direction – from oligarch to criminal.

The third reason has to do with Putin's return to Moscow. It's pretty obvious that the organisers of the operation, whoever they were, had intended the president to return to a victory but, if that could not be managed in time, at least after the battle had passed its most heated phase. But he arrived in the thick of things and was drawn into the battle personally. This was not anticipated in the script and was not in the president's interest – despite his sympathies. In other words, what these people should have done, rather than settling for a protracted and uncertain siege, was to have stormed the fortress immediately.

And now to the lessons of the 'insurrection':

● Despite all the talk about the Russian state's power over information, our authorities lack it. The control of information wielded by any government (even in a society that is relatively democratic) is only the sum of support for those authorities by the majority of the national media or the population as a whole.

- Specialists in public relations are more influential than state agencies, even when both act in a professional way which they certainly didn't do in this conflict. Law and journalism are both public professions and the investigator is only an investigator. In terms of public relations, the procurator's office was, quite simply, routed. Our state agencies are mere children when it comes to spin.
- Putin has no qualified team (that may be less his personal problem than the problem of the state as a whole); Gusinsky does.
- Public relations is at least as important as the story itself. Everyone knew this even before Gusinsky was arrested. Everyone, that is, except our officials whose natural tendency is to work in secret.
- The media have long been the fourth estate in Russia and, with a weak and downtrodden judicial system, they could be said to have risen to third place in the heirarchy in terms of power.
- In Russia, a media empire is pure politics. The oil industry or any other business interest, simply has a little politics mixed in with the oil or whatever. They could have bundled any oil magnate into prison with barely a fraction of the trouble over Gusinsky.
- For the West, and in many ways for us, freedom of expression is a 'sacred cow' – even when the books do get cooked sometimes. It's no coincidence that when he commented on the affair, President Clinton effectively called Gusinsky 'a member of the journalistic profession'.
- In the stand-off between the Kremlin and Gusinsky/Malashenko [a senior figure in NTV] we saw their profound ideological incompatibility. The Kremlin thinks in terms of nation states; the owners of NTV in terms of international corporations without borders. In many ways, both sides were sincere in what they did and said. For Putin and the Kremlin, Russia has interests outside and beyond the West; for Gusinsky and Malashenko, these interests do not exist.
- Why didn't people – the active sector of the population – cheer the arrest of an oligarch? Because even the state of sin in which we now live is sweeter than the virtue of our lives in the past (if that is what it was). Because Gusinsky in prison became a symbol of the suppressed hope of hundreds of thousands of people to get rich.
- Why did the intelligentsia – which has long been competing with the public to expose the oligarchs – come out in support of Gusinsky? While the public get nothing from the oligarchs, the ranks of the intelligentsia feed on him. There is no more egotistical group in Russian

society than the intelligentsia. Another sector of the intelligentsia – forever with its mind concentrated on the 'good' in the midst of this evil world in which it is forced to live – finds a way out of this paradox by dividing evil (the oligarchic system) into personalised carriers of good and evil. This ensures a comfortable life as well as psychological and philosophical well-being. A third group gave Gusinsky its support because it never trusts the authorities – especially when the authorities fail to feed them as they did in the days of the USSR. In addition, westernisers, the most active if not the biggest detachment of the intelligentsia, stepped in on behalf of a westerniser out of a (frequently not unfounded) fear of everything that is Russian – that is to say in the historical, rather than ethnic, sense.

● The Kremlin undermined its own position through its lack of transparency: it revealed its methods but hid its aims. Media-MOST didn't hide its aims: its own survival and the desire to get the news out to the public. Worthy and understandable aims even if there was a certain lack of sincerity. For this reason, nobody bothered to examine their methods any further – much as the federal troops managed to do in Chechnya, and for which Media-MOST criticised them. The Kremlin failed to get its message across, leaving the field open to Media-MOST. And so the story, given the spin, became one of repression for reporting the truth. But since this might have appeared self-centred and trivial, the threat to Media-MOST was expanded to take in the whole of society: free speech was about to be liquidated.

I still believe the assault on Gusinsky was political (which the Kremlin has been afraid to admit), not because of what Media-MOST wrote or showed on NTV – others have done the same – but because the Kremlin sees Gusinsky's empire as a serious political opposition that challenges the state in some of its activities, and is increasingly slipping out of Russian jurisdiction while remaining active in the Russian political arena. The Kremlin categorises MOST as a radical political proto-party, in opposition, acting under the guise of a media group. There's a good deal to be said for this view, particularly the iron discipline that reigns in Gusinsky's empire and its collaboration with political rather than business figures in Russia and the rest of the world.

But in a democratic society it is illegal to punish people for 'doing politics', even if they do challenge the status quo. If no one is hurling bombs at state officials, it is extremely difficult to prove that political activity is 'anti-state'. And the search for a purely criminal charge with which to incriminate someone is almost a lost cause. Politics float up to the surface automatically and then you get what we very nearly got: 'the persecution of dissidents'.

Media–MOST is not a stronghold of democracy in Russia. It is not even an essential element within it. Democracy needs, depends on, the entire structure of an independent media as we have it at the moment and in which MOST, and NTV in particular, play a leading role.

Nor is the Kremlin, or even the procurator's office, the main threat to democracy in Russia. They are, however, essential elements in a state structure, including a democratic one (though the procurator's office needs to be reformed and its standards raised). Furthermore, all these bodies – the Kremlin, the procurator's office, NTV – are overwhelmingly staffed by Russian citizens and residents. So it is in all our interests that both these 'insurrections' should extinguish each other. The country doesn't need them. ❏

Vitaly Tretyakov is the editor of Nezavisimaya gazeta, *a member of the Berezovsky media group. This is an edited version of the article that appeared in the paper on 20 June*
Translated by Irena Maryniak

This sporting life

A whirlwind of global capital has engulfed the sporting world. Gone are its lofty ideals and ethical concerns, replaced by the collusion of money and the media that sweeps scandals under the carpet and keeps the lid on dirt

File compiled by Tony Callaghan and Henderson Mullin

MIKE MARQUSEE

This sporting lie

Though't be a sportful combat
Yet in the trial much opinion dwells
William Shakespeare, *Troilus and Cressida*

The sports explosion of the last years of the twentieth century is hailed as a success story, a triumph of globalisation. But there have been losers as well as winners; and among the losers may be found both loathers and lovers of sport and, perhaps, sport itself. Amid the clamorous hyperbole emanating from the global sports industry, it's hard to remember that it all begins as play, that these exertions emerge from humanity's childhood, from the spontaneous but structured interaction of the human body with balls, sticks, baskets and tree stumps.

In April 2000, representatives of the key players in the global sports industry assembled in London for 'Sport Business 2000', a high-powered conference organised by Dow Jones, the investment broker and financial analyst, and Sport Business International, an online magazine. Among the participants were international governing bodies (the International Olympic Committee and the Federation of International Football Associations), major broadcasters (Sky TV and Turner Sports), sponsors (Nike, Coca-Cola), specialist sports marketers, events managers and agents (International Management Group), investment bankers, stadium architects, Internet enterprises (Yahoo, Sportal and sports.com) and not a few of the 1,000 consultancies said to be lubricating the sports sponsorship market, now worth US$20 billion annually – up from a paltry US$500,000 30 years ago. There were, however, no sports stars. The price of admission to the conference was £1,250 (cUS$2,000) per delegate, plus VAT. Not a great deal to pay for the inside track in an industry that accounts for something like two per cent of GDP in the

United States, Europe, Japan and Australia, and looks like getting bigger by the year.

Topics discussed at the conference included the impact of new technology, the difficulties of managing intellectual property rights in a global marketplace, the commercial potential of new multi-use stadiums equipped with interactive 'smart seats', and the relative merits of event versus broadcast sponsorship, on-site versus virtual advertising, cross-corporate convergence versus specialisation and niche-marketing.

Intriguingly, one seminar was entitled, 'How can investors reconcile sport's inherent uncertainties?' After all, the team you sponsor may not win the cup, the athlete who endorses your product may crack a vertebra. One answer to the conundrum came that very week from South Africa, where cricket captain Hansie Cronje confessed to accepting bribes from bookmakers. More than most sports, cricket has remained wedded to the lofty rhetoric of sport's higher purpose, the enduring but ill-defined ethos of 'fair play'. Cronje's fall from grace was, therefore, the cue for anguished laments for lost innocence on leader pages in several continents.

In itself, the presence of bookmakers in the game is an old story. Cricket evolved in the eighteenth century from a folk pastime to a modern spectator sport under the impetus of the high stakes wagered by cash-flush British aristocrats. In their quest for high-return speculative investments, they staged the matches, employed the players, put up the stakes and bet profligately on the results. What is new today is the larger economic and social context. Satellite television and multinational media conglomerates have transformed the economic value of international cricket. In South Asia, the game's largest market, cricket has elbowed aside just about every other sporting activity, and nothing captures the public imagination (and lures the punters) more than a Pakistan v India clash. Some US$6 billion a year is said to be wagered on matches played in India alone. Meanwhile, thanks to the convergence of a deregulated financial regime and the spread of information technology, money flows from one account to another with blithe disregard for national boundaries or legal niceties.

In this environment the illegal bookmaking syndicates have flourished. They are merely the dark underside of globalisation, and only one of a number of powerful forces seeking to exploit the huge popular base of South Asian cricket. Corporate sponsors, advertising and

Fans protests against Rupert Murdoch's purchase bid for Manchester United –
Credit: Clive Brunskill/Allsports

marketing agencies, media empires, government bureaucrats, politicians
and demagogues – all have an investment in the game, and all seek to
shape it to their own ends, to 'reconcile sport's inherent uncertainties'.
As a result, international cricket in South Asia has become something of
a three-ring circus of corporate, national and individual self-
aggrandisement, a victim of the spread of a market-driven culture of
cynicism, hype and hustle. As individual financial success is elevated

above all other aspirations, there is ever greater acceptance of the ethics of the quick fix, the fast buck and the big score. In cricket, as elsewhere, customary ethical inhibitions have been swept away by the whirlwind of capital.

The questions raised by the match-fixing revelations – about the governance of global sport, about the authenticity of the spectacle – are by no means confined to cricket. Football, rugby, athletics, tennis, boxing, baseball, not to mention the Olympics – all have been tainted by controversies arising from conflicts of interest and commercial pressures. In the clamour surrounding big-money sports, the voices of the fans, of the grassroots participants whose voluntary exertions provide the base of the pyramid, are rarely heard. Democratic debate is drowned amid the Babel of vested interests; scrutiny of the industry's inner workings is confined to the margins. Behind this crisis of governance and credibility lies the powerful and intricately interconnected corporate-media-sport nexus on display at the Sport Business 2000 conference. This nexus buys and sells sport, ever striving to reduce its refractory human complexity to commodity status. In doing so, it is changing the very look and feel of the world we share, and the way we share it.

Sport today is being used to 'brand' ever-expanding acres of public space – material, televisual and cyber. 'The marks of international sports events have become extremely valuable properties,' explains Gerhard Proschoka, 'the visible expression of the link between supporters and events are an effective way of giving products added value.' Proschoka is head of licensing at ISL, a successful sports marketing agency, which, on FIFA's behalf, flogged more than 300 licences for 1998 World Cup-branded merchandise. Since retail sales amounted to some US$1.2 billion, Proschoka must be right about the 'added value'.

The single most powerful individual within the corporate-media-sport nexus must be Rupert Murdoch, whose diverse portfolio gives him a stake in nearly every aspect of the industry. Murdoch has explained his strategy frankly. He regards sports as a 'battering ram' to enter and capture emergent markets. His Fox, Sky and Star TV networks broadcast major sporting events across North America, Europe and Asia, and is now collaborating with Globo, the biggest cable broadcaster in South America. Murdoch's newspapers in Britain, the US, Australia and the Far East report on his televised sporting events, and he is not reluctant to take advantage of this convenient 'synergy'. He also has direct holdings in sporting institutions themselves – British and German football clubs, major league baseball teams, rugby league clubs in Australia. Recently, he has begun investing in the Internet, and has signed an agreement with Yahoo. In Asia, Murdoch's Star has joined forces with ESPN (Entertainment and Sports Programming Network) to carve up the sports market. ESPN boasts 20 television networks (including Euro-Sport) spanning 182 countries. It also runs the leading sports website in North America, where one-third of all Internet use is said to be sports-related. ESPN is owned by the Disney Corporation, which also controls the ABC television network as well as major league baseball's Anaheim Angels and an ice hockey team christened the Mighty Ducks, after the Disney film of the same name. The bigger the investment in sport, the greater the temptation to exercise hands-on management. Murdoch and Disney are part of a trend towards increasing cross-ownership among media, sponsors and sports entities. The Italian politician television magnate Silvio Berlusconi is the principal owner of AC Milan and has a major stake in Sportal (the British-based Internet sports company). Canal Plus, the French pay-TV station, owns Paris St-Germain football club. Fiat owns not only the Juventus football club but also the Ferrari Formula One motor-racing squad. Euromedia TV, the German media group, now controls 50% of Formula One itself. Nike's contract with the Brazil football federation gives it a major role in determining where and when the national team plays, and even, some whisper, who gets to play in it. As media empires and sponsors increasingly seek control and even ownership of sporting institutions, these institutions encroach into media and merchandising. Manchester United and the New York Yankees, perhaps the world's most valuable sports 'brands', have both expanded into Internet and media business, and even into other sports. As a result of all this increasing interconnectedness, whose purpose is to maximise profit from sport, and minimise the risks posed their 'inherent uncertainties', special interests call the shots; accountability and transparency go by the wayside; deals are struck under a veil of secrecy and the public – aka the fans – are increasingly marginalised and outpriced when it comes to getting a ticket for their local team.

The 'level playing field' beloved of the architects of the current world economic order is, of course, a metaphor from sport. But in an irony characteristic of the age, the level playing field imposed by global capital seems to be having a distinctly unlevelling impact on the sports field itself. The concentrations of wealth and power now driving the industry are generating new inequalities within sports, between sports, and among sporting nations. Scores of traditional and indigenous pastimes, as well as once-vital modern sporting sub-cultures such as West Indies cricket, Welsh rugby and Cuban boxing, are being pushed to the margins, and threatened with extinction. In South Asia, hockey has been overwhelmed by cricket; in England, cricket is being overwhelmed by football. What future awaits curling in Scotland, wrestling houses in Iran, *elle* in Sri Lanka or *kabbadi* in India?

The impact of globalisation on sport's labour force is immediately apparent to anyone watching Chelsea or the New York Yankees. Major league baseball now recruits much of its talent from the Caribbean and South America; a multinational labour force is placed at the service of an overwhelmingly dominant North American market. Some North American players ply their trade in Japan, but there is no migration southwards – at least not since the flow of black ball players dried up after Jackie Robinson broke the colour bar in 1947. Likewise, most African athletes who hope to shine on the world stage pursue their careers at North American colleges, and African footballers seek their fortunes in Europe (and also Turkey, India and Japan).

According to the 'rich list' compiled by Deloitte-Touche, all 20 of the world's wealthiest football clubs are now based in Europe. Long-established South American clubs with massive fan bases, like Flamengo of Brazil, have fallen down the list as satellite and cable cash flows into the big western European leagues. In South America, cable hook-ups remain confined to a small elite (only 3.3 per cent in Brazil) and clubs are forced to boost income by selling players to Europe. The European matches in which the local heroes play are then telecast back to South America, reinforcing the superior status of European over local football.

During the 1990s, global expenditure on sports sponsorship trebled. But the distribution of this growth was highly imbalanced. In 1998, 37.8% of this sum was spent in North America, 36.4% in Europe and 20.8% in Asia, with South America way behind and Africa virtually out of the reckoning. What counts here is not just the size of TV audiences, but their relative disposable income. The CAF, the African football championship, is followed passionately by hundreds of millions, but, alas, as far as corporate sponsors are concerned, there's little profit to be made, and African football, for all its wealth of talent, remains an underdeveloped, shoestring affair.

Even in the developed world, the distribution of the spoils is highly unequal. In 1998, sports sponsorship in the UK was worth £350 million (cUS$525), two-thirds of which was consumed by football and Formula One. Other sports are being marginalised, as are women's sports. A survey revealed that 82% of companies involved in sports sponsorship said they were 'not interested' in women's sports, although 57% conceded that they would be interested if there was greater 'sex appeal'.

Increasing disparities in wealth are also compromising the integrity of sporting competitions. The pursuit of ever greater TV audiences led to a rapid expansion of major league baseball franchises and the adoption of a 'souped up' ball more likely to fly out of the stadium. The result has been lopsided competition and the devaluation of the home run. The fate of the FA Cup, the prototype modern spring competition, reflects similar pressures. As a handful of rich clubs outspend their competitors off the field, the spectacle on the field becomes more predictable and therefore less compelling. The giant-killing feats that once tingled the collective spine are becoming rarer. In the past, a Cup encounter between old rivals would always outdraw a league encounter. Now the reverse is the case. The Premiership has evolved into a glamorous, exclusive coterie, and the European champions league outshines all else. The symbolic eclipse of the FA Cup was the withdrawal in 1999-2000 of the Cup holders, Manchester United, who preferred instead to take part in a 'world club' competition with no pedigree. In this they were backed by the British government, which saw the Manchester United move as a boost for the country's bid to host the 2006 World Cup. For both the football club and the politicians, conquering global markets took precedence over preserving a long-established national institution.

The money flooding into sport has raised its social status, and with that rising status has come ticket-price inflation, the growth of the corporate hospitality industry and the colonisation of sports arenas by luxury boxes. Everywhere, sports fans from lower income groups are finding it harder to gain access to live sporting events, and are becoming more dependent on satellite and cable television providers for their regular dose of what used to be known as a popular pastime. According to the 1998 British Social Trends Report, during a three-month period one-third of those surveyed in the top bracket ABC categories had attended a live spectator sports event. In contrast, only 18% of Ds had attended one and only seven per cent of Es. In the last baseball World Series, only 5,000 seats, ten per cent of the total, were placed on sale to members of the public in New York City. Concerns about the high cost of attending matches in Japan during the 2002 World Cup met with a casual rebuff from Lennart Johansson, chair of FIFA's World Cup organising committee. 'When it comes to the cost for the fans, they have to look in their wallets to see whether they can afford it or not.'

As the new Internet, mobile phone and digital platform technology evolve and spread, 'an already sports rich world will become even richer', predicts sportbusiness.com. 'Sport will be available on demand in the home, the office and even the car. Technology will make sport yet more international and that, in turn, will accelerate the development of truly global sporting super-brands with a devoted world wide audience.' But this global audience will be fragmented and segmented as never before. The greater flexibility of the medium will enable greater targeting of the product. One way or another, pay-per-view will become the norm. Sport will increasingly become part of that ceaseless, seamless flow of imagery and information that floats like a veil between individuals and the life they share with larger communities. Ideal, no doubt, for promoting the products of multinational corporations. But what will be left of the common experience of watching sport as part of a crowd, with all its biases, tensions and banter, its collective passions and heated arguments? For all their cultural differences and mutual ignorance, this was an experience that united sports fans across the globe, and out of it grew a wide variety of popular sporting cultures. In its heyday, modern sport helped bring strangers together; it helped forge new urban and even national communities. Sometimes, in some places, it still plays that role. But these days as often as not it atomises communities and eviscerates collective identities.

Last year, the World Wrestling Federation was floated on the stock exchange for US$1.5 billion. Financial analysts who predicted the move would raise half that amount should have known better. In 1999, more than half the top 60 pay-per-view events in the USA were produced by WWF or one of its affiliates. Head-to-head with the Michael Jordan-less NBA play-offs, WWF outdrew the glamour sport of the 90s by two to one. WWF also runs one of the top three sports-related websites, with 1.6 million visitors in a single month. Then there's the merchandise, the PlayStations and the videos, not to mention the WWF themed hotel and casino in Las Vegas.

With substantial cable or satellite audiences in every continent, WWF may be, after the Olympics and the football World Cup, the closest thing to a genuinely global sport. Except, of course, that it is not a sport. The outcome is determined and the action is rehearsed in advance – which is why no one will take a bet on a WWF match. Here the 'uncertainties inherent in sport' have been entirely eliminated. WWF is soap opera cast in the form of a perpetual sporting competition. Increasingly, with its commentators and pundits, technical jargon, pouting, preening superstars, super slo-mo TV replays, vendettas, grudge matches and spurious controversies, it resembles a gothic parody of big-time modern sport. WWF founder and owner Vince Macmahon has even had himself and his family written into the scripts, which enact the now familiar conflict between superstars and sports bosses.

In WWF, victory and defeat, the goodies and the baddies, the twists and turns of sporting contests, come ready packaged, like junk food, and like junk food, their appeal crosses borders with only token resistance. Ironically, WWF and its imitators build on – and ultimately displace – a wide variety of indigenous and traditional combat-based entertainments. Only a generation ago the wrestler Dada Singh was a hero to children and adults alike across north India. Today he would have to sign up with Macmahon or Turner or one of their global competitors if he wanted to reach even his own home audience. The rebirth of this fairground entertainment through the medium of a globalised economy and technology – and its funhouse mirror image of modern sport – is testimony not merely to the enduring popular taste for blood and thunder, but also to the increasing reduction of modern sport to an endless parade of packaged simulacra. The signifiers of modern sport have been detached from lived experience to float in a 'virtual' reality owned and designed by a private corporation.

Although it is entirely contrived from above, the WWF spectacle gives free rein to the most ferocious expressions of partisanship. Identities, loyalties and affinities that football or baseball clubs acquire over many years are market-researched, briskly manufactured and shamelessly promoted. Strangely, one reason for the appeal of WWF seems to be the very nakedness of its artifice. In merrily discarding the higher ethos of sport and 'fair play', it seems less mealy-mouthed, less hypocritical, than many 'legitimate' sports.

Artificially hyped collective antagonisms are certainly not confined to working-class attractions like boxing and pro-wrestling. The Olympics have become a peculiarly noxious cocktail of national chauvinism and global capitalism. Even upmarket events like the traditionally genteel Ryder Cup golf contest between Europe and America have erupted in overheated jingoism. And corporate sponsors and broadcasters alike now have a vested interest in hyping the India-Pakistan cricket rivalry to the limit – and beyond. Earlier this year, as the two teams faced each other in Australia, their governments were exchanging mutual threats of nuclear annihilation, not to mention actual gunfire in disputed Kashmir. Murdoch, Disney and the soft-drinks sponsors saw fit to promote this sporting encounter as *Qayamat* – apocalypse.

Perhaps the crowning irony of the contemporary media–corporate–sport nexus is that it has turned the over-inflated response to national sporting success and failure into a global phenomenon. The mood swings that have long characterised the inner life of the sports fan have been transformed into a public mania, manipulated for commercial and political advantage. One of the pleasures of Nick Hornby's *Fever Pitch* is that it never forgets that sporting partisanship, the habit of linking one's individual fate to that of a team or performer, is fundamentally absurd. For true sports lovers, 'sport's inherent uncertainties' are its deepest attractions; they are what drove generations of spectators and supporters through the turnstiles. The fans' *amour fou* has always been tragicomic, but the huge investments and excessive importance now attached to sport are coarsening the drama. The justification of sport is that it is a harmless diversion, an end in itself. Those forces that subordinate it to other ends (the conquest and exploitation of markets) now threaten to ruin this delightfully trivial, yet somehow endlessly creative, exercise of human faculties. ❏

Mike Marqusee's most recent book is Redemption Song: Muhammad Ali and the Spirit of the Sixties *(Verso). He is a leading campaigner against racism in sport and is chair of Hit Racism for Six*

GARRY WHANNEL

Stars in whose eyes?

Politicians and moral crusaders want sports stars as role models for youth in an age of 'moral decline'. But the media's more interested in scandal and laddishnesss than in sober folk heroes

We seem a long way from the days when sport was regarded as character building. Recent events in the world of sport include England footballer David Beckham giving a one-fingered gesture to England fans, who were reportedly yelling 'your wife is a whore' and 'I hope your son dies of cancer'. Beckham was then criticised in sections of the media for behaving like a yob. Shortly after that match, the governing body of European football threatened to throw England out of the Euro 2000 tournament if there were any more riotous scenes involving English fans. At the same time, South African cricket captain Hansie Cronje revealed he had accepted money to fix the result of cricket matches.

Another former role model, Mike Tyson, arrived to fight in Glasgow, only to be met by women's groups lobbying for his expulsion from the country. The black ex-world heavyweight champion still denies the rape for which he was jailed.

A few weeks earlier, the obituaries of Stanley Matthews had proclaimed him 'the last gentleman of soccer' – a model sportsman – quiet, reflective, modest, reserved and courteous, and from humble origins. He was a genius, an artist; never booked, he was totally dedicated and had rigorous self-discipline. This was contrasted with today's overpaid superstars.

Elite sport now constitutes a key component of popular culture. The stars of sport have become celebrities whose fame extends beyond the confines of track or field. Globalisation and capitalisation have made major sport a lucrative international industry. Large financial rewards and the pressures to succeed have encouraged violence, gamesmanship, corruption and the use of performance-enhancing drugs.

Those who would like to see top sports stars as role models bewail their tendency to behave badly and contrast the era when sportsmen (supposedly) behaved like gentlemen with the modern era of 'pampered stars with Ferraris, showbiz lifestyles and million-pound homes'. Images of sports stars have become the focal point of a discourse about supposed 'moral decline' that is distinctly conservative in character, counterposing as it does a supposedly corrupt present with an imagined noble past. Modern sports stars, though, are products of a media-rich age in which sport itself has been transformed.

Since Stanley Matthews won his FA Cup Final medal in 1953, the growth of television coverage has transformed sport. During the 1960s and 1970s, a series of technical innovations – video recording, video editing, action replay, slow motion, colour, communication satellites, lightweight cameras – turned television sport into a spectacular product. The audience came to expect full-colour live images of major sport from around the world. Direct television revenue was important, but television also unlocked the possibilities of advertising and sponsorship. Sponsorship grew rapidly through the 1970s and 1980s.

The new medium meant that the faces of top stars became familiar to a widening public. Fringe earnings of stars began to rival their main on-field earnings. Sports agents grew in power, with entrepreneurs like Jack Kramer, Mark McCormack, Kerry Packer, Donald Dell and Horst Dassler challenging and sometimes usurping the power of the established governing bodies. The launch of satellite television at the end of the 1980s marked the beginning of a new era, in which dedicated sports channels, available on a pay-per-channel basis, further increased the amount of sport on television and in the case of football and a few major events the amount that television paid for it.

In Britain, BSkyB broadcasts over 25,000 hours of sport a year – around eight times as much as the five terrestrial channels combined. Acquiring live rights to Premier League football saved the company from financial collapse, and established pay-per-channel and pay-per-view as viable, indeed lucrative, propositions. The success of subscription sports channels on BSkyB and the more aggressive competition for the television rights to major events have undermined the long-established dominance of the BBC in television sport.

In battles to win and hold on to audiences, the presence of top stars, figures that the audience could identify with, became crucial. Television's intimacy, its focus on the face, and chat-based modes of presentation, served to establish stars as personalities; they were increasingly the subject of scandal, in part because of the tabloidisation of the press.

The purchase of the *Sun* by Rupert Murdoch, and its relaunch as a tabloid in 1969, triggered a tabloid revolution in which the *Daily Mirror* and the *Sun* competed for the working-class reader with more explicit pin-ups, sport and scandal. Many of the stories involving drink, drugs, sex or violence in which stars such as George Best, Alex Higgins, Ian Botham, Paul Gascoigne and Stan Collymore featured in stories that might well not have made it into the pages in an earlier era when sports journalists often knew what went on, but were complicit in protecting the reputation of those they were close to. By the 1980s, however, sports stars were front-page material and it was not sports journalists but general news reporters who were in the forefront of this erosion of the boundary between public and private.

In a culture that is self-referential, parodic and marked by the high-speed globalised circulation of images, the role of the sporting hero is inevitably subject to public deconstruction. In the world of post-modernity where surface appearance dominates substance, sports stars become more like the characters in a soap opera – no more or less 'real'. It is notable that three of the most prominent sports stars in the news in recent years – Magic Johnson, OJ Simpson and Mike Tyson – have all been newsworthy for reasons largely unconnected with sport.

Yet there is still a clear yearning for heroics, as can be seen in the celebratory portrayals of new stars such as Michael Owen or Tiger Woods. Those who look to sports stars as role models are more likely to favour a figure like Woods or Alan Shearer – good-looking, conventional, and mind-numbingly dull. Yet for the public and media generally, the quiet, unflamboyant public style of a Stanley Matthews is no longer sufficient – note the relative lack of interest in champion boxer Lennox Lewis, and the perception of Tim Henman and Greg Rusedski as rather dull, whereas controversial figures like Chris Eubank, Prince Naseem and Vinnie Jones inspire anger and hostility, but also grab media

Liverpool striker Robbie Fowler expressing support for sacked dock workers after a european match. Fowler was later fined by UEFA – Credit: Mike Cooper/Allsports

attention.

There is massive and misplaced faith in the idea that leading sporting figures can be role models. It rests on a rather quaint and old-fashioned model of the relation between young people and media images. The young audience is much more sophisticated than those who call for role models appear to believe. They are perfectly able to distinguish between those moments when a footballer produces sublime skill (Gascoigne's goal against Scotland in 1996) and those moments when a footballer behaves like a fool (Gascoigne having tequila cocktails squirted down his throat in the 'dentist's chair'). The desperation for sports stars to be role models reflects a loss in influence of other more traditional sources of moral guidance – teachers, parents and priests.

David Beckham may be a simple figure but his image is complex and malleable. He has attracted unprecedented barracking because he was sent off in a key World Cup game for an unnecessary foul; because he plays for Manchester United whose richness, arrogance and dominance of English football has produced a jealous hatred; because he is married to a pop singer; and because he is perceived as having deviated from the narrow confines of mainstream masculinity in his dress styles. He is also England's one undisputed world-class player. There is a certain type of fan who is made deeply uncomfortable by Beckham's ability to personify everything (wealth, glamour, grace) that he will never have.

In public discussion of sport and stars, though, there is considerable confusion: sports stars are not moral teachers – they have no more responsibility to set a good example than do pop stars. What they are is entertainers and what they do have is a responsibility to entertain us. So we are more engaged by the exploits of the bad boys of this world – we may not approve but, in significant numbers, we buy the papers to read about them, and ring phone-ins to discuss them. Expectations of sports stars should be scaled down: we should not expect them to be role models. We can, however, insist that they are honest, and ruthlessly bar those exposed as corrupt.

The Cronje revelations shock in part because they concern a sport that appears as a pastoral redoubt – a last-ditch defence of purity in a corrupt world – the players even wear white. Yet here we have a captain, no mere peripheral figure, confessing, not to a sudden inexplicable lapse, a 'moment of madness', but to systematic corruption over a period of years. It's not cricket.

The Cronje revelations could yet turn out to be a very good thing; if they force sport to confront an evil it has been all too keen to sweep under the carpet. It would be a healthy sign if journalists and politicians were more concerned over bribery, corruption and shady financial dealings, and less ready to be whipped up into a moral panic over a player giving a one-fingered salute. ❏

Garry Whannel is professor of media cultures at the University of Luton and is completing a book on sports stars to be published by Routledge

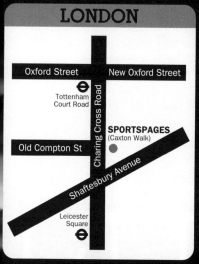
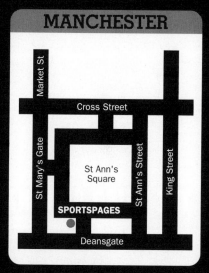

BANNED SPORTS

THE VENETIAN REGATTA, traditionally meant be a celebration of community feeling, was suppressed in the 14th century for creating divisions amongst the citizens'.

ULTIMATE FIGHTING, the 'mixed' martial arts competition in which opponents can box and kick, is banned in Illinois, Michigan, New York, Ohio, Oklahoma and Wisconsin.

CHEESE-ROLLING was banned in Gloucestershire after 33 competitors were injured in 1997. The 200-year-old annual race was re-instated in 1999, and there were no serious injuries.

FOOTBALL was banned in 1389 by Richard II of England because it interfered with archery practice; later monarchs continued to ban the sport into the 15th century, to little effect.

SURFING was banned by European missionaries in 1821 who thought it immoral. It was not officially revived until 1920, when a famous Hawaiian swimmer, Duke Kahanamoku, formed the first surfing club in Waikiki.

SUMO WRESTLING was banned as a spectator sport by Japanese shoguns in the 12th century; public matches were not revived until the early 17th century when it became the Japanese national sport.

HURLING was prohibited in Ireland after the 12th century Norman invasion.

LIVE PIGEON SHOOTING was replaced by the clay variety in competitive events throughout Europe in the second half of the 20th century.

'HANDGUN SPORTS will no longer be practiced on the mainland of Britain' Home Secretary Jack Straw told the Commons, when he announced the Labour government's 1997 ban on ownership and use of pistols. This followed a public outcry after the shootings of 16 children and their teacher in a primary school in Dunblane in 1996. 100,000 British shooters had their sport abolished overnight. However, in a controversial move the Home Office recently announced 'special dispensation' to allow pistol events at the 2002 Commonwealth Games, due to be held in Manchester. Failure to bend the law would have ended any hope of Britain hosting future Commonwealth or Olympic Games. ❑

JOHN HOBERMAN

Behind the mask

All is not as it seems in the racially integrated world of sport: harmony hides a world of exclusion and inequality

The global prominence of African and African-American athletes represents for many people a clear example of racial progress in the modern world. Here, after all, is an international subculture in which black people can assert themselves and enjoy success to a degree that makes the world of sport look like an interracial utopia. Compared to other venues of competition and endeavour, such as business, science or the law, the sports world is, in fact, an extraordinary social phenomenon that seems to contradict some familiar racial stereotypes. The sheer celebrity of the black athletic star appears to be a refutation of the colonial anonymity of the black masses, his wealth contrasts with traditional images of black poverty, while his honoured status appears to dissolve centuries of racial subordination. The utopian potential of sport in this sense has long intrigued the African-American leader Jesse Jackson. Describing the stadium crowd at a US professional football game, he marvels that there is 'no suggestion of racial tension. Why is that possible there but not in the church, or in the schools, or anywhere else? Because whenever the playing field is even, and the rules are public and the goals are clear, we can all move to the next level ... We want an even playing field.'

The past century of integrated sport has demonstrated that interracial athletic competition has both positive and negative effects. The sports world does present a model of racial integration that makes more comprehensive social reforms easier for many people to imagine. It has provided many black people around the world with opportunities for social and economic advancement. It has also provided a platform for a small number of courageous black athletes to demand racial reforms in the larger societies to which they belong.

But it is also important to recognise the limits to progress that apply within this interracial domain. Racial integration in the sports world is relatively easy precisely because, as Jesse Jackson suggests, the more intractable social problems are left outside the stadium. At the administrative level, moreover, the colonial racial hierarchy remains quite intact. The blacks who currently wield influence in the International Olympic Committee (IOC) and the international sports federations can be counted on the fingers of one hand: Anita deFrantz (IOC), Keba Mbaye (IOC), Lamine Diack (IAAF). Of the ten members who were expelled or resigned from the IOC in 1999, a conspicuous number were black Africans who lacked the political connections that might have saved them. But when the powerful European soccer official Lennart Johannson made a racist remark about black Africans in 1996, he retained his position.

The upward mobility and wealth achieved by the most successful black athletes dominates media coverage and promotes an illusory sense of social advancement for blacks as a group. Who would guess, in a world of National Basketball Association millionaires, that the net worth of the average African-American home is only one-tenth that of its white counterpart? In similar vein, omnipresent images of vigorous black athletes help to camouflage the disastrous health problems of both African and African-American populations. One black superstar can put a happy face on an entire system of racial injustice. Even a conscientious and politically progressive figure like Pelé – one of the few elite athletes ever to serve as a government minister – has inadvertently distracted public attention from the enormous racial inequities that characterise Brazilian society; the sensational feats of Kenyan runners displace coverage of the political tyranny that is destroying their society.

The social costs and failures associated with racially integrated sport have been underestimated precisely because they cannot function as signs and portents of the racial progress globalisation requires. The racial integration of European soccer, for example, has been accompanied by many racist manifestations that raise troubling questions about the social utility of multiracial sport. A spokesman for the German Soccer Federation said in 1995, for example, that his sport stood for 'problem-free integration.' But what sport symbolises does not always match the reality inside the stadium. In years past, black soccer players in German stadiums would hear calls of 'Hush, hush, hush, nigger in the bush!' or watch as bananas rained down on the field. More recently, it has been good form for a German team to have at least one African player, but the effects of such initiatives are not clear. Charles Friedek, a German triple-jumper who is the son of an African-American father and a German mother, commented last year: 'We [blacks] can win medals for them, but they won't let us in. When they see us in the stadium in our athletics clothes, they cheer us. If we walk on the street in our athletics clothes, then they think of us as asylum-seekers.' Generations of African-American athletes (and soldiers) have made the same discovery about their own tenuous civic status, no matter how many medals they won 'for their country.'

These racial problems exist across Europe. The Dutch national soccer team includes important black players from Surinam whose relations with their white teammates have at times been contentious. In Italy, one black player was hanged in effigy inside the stadium, and another subjected to other forms of racist abuse when he was on the field. 'We are disgusted, not only by the poor idiots who reject Ze Maria on account of his skin colour, but even more by the silent masses around them,' *Gazzetta dello Sport* commented. In some European stadiums, the spectators screech like chimpanzees at the sight of a black player. Racial integration inside the stadium remains essentially symbolic: athletic stardom is not equivalent to fully human status, let alone equal social status, in the eyes of many Europeans.

This implicit distinction between the black athlete and the fellow citizen has been exploited by the extreme right in France. The National Front politician Jean-Marie Le Pen attracted international attention in 1996 when he told his followers that the multiracial French national soccer team could not really represent France because it included too many 'foreigners.' These athletes, he complained, either did not know how to sing the national anthem or did not sing it 'lustily' like the (all-white) teams of certain other nations.

More ominously, Le Pen has invoked the idea of racial athletic aptitude to justify a racial hierarchy that subordinates blacks. The 1996 Olympic Games, for example, had shown that 'there was an obvious inequality between the black and white races'. The neo-fascist newspaper *Rivarol* mocks the idea that soccer in France might become a 'wonderful laboratory for integration'.

Le Pen's simplistic racial theory of genetically programmed black runners and white swimmers is one example of how multiracial sport has given 19th-century racial anthropology a new lease on life. As Franz Fanon pointed out in *Black Skin, White Masks* (1952), western racism has always identified black people with their bodies to an extraordinary degree. For this reason, stereotypes of black athletic superiority are now firmly established as the most recent version of a racial folklore that has spread across the face of the earth over the past two centuries. A corresponding belief in white athletic inferiority pervades popular thinking about racial differences. Such ideas probably do more than anything else in our public lives to encourage the idea that blacks and whites are biologically different in meaningful ways.

Behind its cosmopolitan façade, multiracial sport in the Age of Globalisation retains a number of colonial features, the worst of which is what one Italian sports official has called 'a new slave market' – the importation into Europe of hundreds of black African teenagers as raw material to be tested, trained and most often discarded by European professional soccer teams. Small wonder that stereotypes of 'the African personality' thrive in this milieu. African marathoners, who have enjoyed much success, run 'too anarchistically,' says the Spanish runner Martin Fiz. They must learn to run patiently, says the German coach Dieter Hogen. The Nigerian soccer team, a British sportswriter comments, 'has the force, the ability, the courage that belies African disorganisation'. Rather than neutralizing such ideas, the multiracial sports world acts as a megaphone that amplifies and broadcasts racial folklore of this kind to an international audience that has already become accustomed to all-black sprint finals and the overwhelming superiority of East African distance runners.

The colonial dynamics of international sport also apply to the relationship between African-American athletes and the predominantly white society that watches, celebrates and sometimes resents them. While African-Americans have believed in sport as an engine of racial progress since the 1920s, the limitations of this strategy have become evident during the period of 'black dominance' in major sports that is now about a generation old. In addition, the African-American athlete has become an international role model whose overwhelming media presence misrepresents African-Americans as a group.

Most of the familiar images of black athletes in the United States do not serve the social advancement of African-Americans. In recent years, black athletes have been involved in a highly publicised series of criminal cases that have begun to worry the white owners of professional teams. The recent banning of a throat-slashing gesture by the National Football League was widely interpreted as an attempt to control the violent impulses of black players. The merging of a showy black athletic style with the crime-ridden 'hip-hop' culture of the popular music industry has further promoted the identification of black athletes with criminal behaviour. This is a significant phenomenon in a society where most whites already believe blacks to be violence-prone by nature.

The social and political activism once practised by African-American sports heroes like Jackie Robinson and Muhammad Ali is defunct. Like the vast majority of elite athletes everywhere, African-American athletes are essentially apolitical. Until his recent and ineffectual endorsement of Bill Bradley's presidential candidacy, Michael Jordan had shown absolutely no interest in political principles or controversy. One black sports columnist has called basketball players 'the most politically oblivious group of athletes' in the United States. While African-American athletes in team sports now have an annual income approaching US$2 billion, their financial contributions to educational institutions have been negligible.

The prominence of black athletes can also affect the educational ambitions of black children. Over-identification with athletes and the world of physical performances limits the development of black children by discouraging academic achievement in favour of physical self-expression. A survey released in 1997 showed that two-thirds of African-American teenagers between the ages of 13 and 18 believed they would be able to support themselves as professional athletes. Another factor driving this syndrome is an intense peer pressure that equates academic excellence with effeminacy and racial disloyalty and identifies 'blackness' with physical prowess. All of these social phenomena demonstrate that it is time to relieve black people everywhere of the athletic identity our colonial legacy has inflicted upon them. ❏

John Hoberman *is a professor at the University of Texas and has written extensively on the social implications of sport. His most recent book is* Darwin's Athletes: how sport has damaged Black America and preserved the myth of race *(Houghton Mifflin)*

JON ENTINE

Breaking the taboo

Uncovering the dominance of black athletes in some sports, and white athletes in others, is a simple matter of consulting the record books – try to explain it and controversy is inevitable

Even a casual mention that significant genetic differences exist between populations can ignite a firestorm. Roger Bannister, who broke the four-minute barrier in the mile and is now a distinguished neurologist and retired Oxford don, was showered with ridicule in 1995 for venturing his opinion 'as a scientist rather than a sociologist' that all athletes are not created equal.

'I am prepared to risk political incorrectness,' said Sir Roger in a speech before the British Association for the Advancement of Science, 'by drawing attention to the seemingly obvious but under-stressed fact that black sprinters and black athletes in general all seem to have certain natural anatomical advantages.'

There are only 800 million blacks, or one in eight of the world population, but athletes of African origin hold every major world running record. In the US, blacks make up 70% of the NFL (National Football League) and 85% of professional basketball. In England, which was slow to allow foreigners into football and has a black population of less than two per cent, one in five soccer players in the Premier League is black.

My book, *Taboo: Why Black Athletes Dominate Sports and Why We Are Afraid to Talk About It*, relates the uncontroversial scientific conclusion that environment and culture alone cannot explain this remarkable phenomenon. 'If you can believe that individuals of recent African ancestry are not genetically advantaged over those of European and Asian ancestry in certain athletic endeavors,' observes Vincent Sarich, biologist at the University of California, Berkeley, 'then you could probably be led to believe just about anything. But such dominance will never convince those whose minds are made up that genetics plays no role in shaping the racial patterns we see in sports. When we discuss issues such as race, it pushes buttons and the cortex just shuts down.'

As equality of opportunity has increased in sports over the past 30 years, equality of results – the diversity of the races of the elite players – has declined. And this is not a black and white issue. Whites of Eurasian ancestry, who have, on average, more natural upper-body strength, predictably dominate weightlifting and field events such as the shot-put and hammer (whites hold 46 of the top 50 throws). Where flexibility is key, East Asians shine, such as in diving and some skating and gymnastic events (hence the term 'Chinese splits'). Blacks of West African ancestry are the premier sprinters and jumpers. East African blacks – Kenyans and Ethiopians in particular – are the world's best distance runners.

Genetically linked, inherited characteristics such as skeletal structure, the distribution of muscle-fibre types, reflex capabilities, metabolic efficiency, lung capacity or the ability to use energy more efficiently, are not evenly distributed across racial groups and cannot be explained by known environmental factors.

But don't expect a dispassionate public discussion of this issue. Since WWII, anthropological orthodoxy has held that the very concept of race is a loaded, social construct. There exists an understandable visceral fear of a slippery slope: if the conclusion drawn from black domination of Olympic track medals is that blacks are physically superior, what is to be made of the enormous over-representation of white Nobel Prize winners?

It was that legitimate concern that energised *Taboo* – my intention to do damage to the racist belief that intelligence and physical ability is somehow inversely connected like a seesaw. Yet, when I attempted to get the book published, I encountered a wall of rejections. Broadly, the reaction was: 'By even suggesting that blacks may have a genetic edge in sports, you are opening up the Pandora's box of intellectual inferiority.'

'You will be accused of spouting old-fashioned racism for even raising the issue of African-American superiority in athletics,' wrote Earl Smith, Chairman of the Department of Sociology at Wake Forest University, a leading black scholar and one of my board members. 'All this beating around the bush has to stop. This is a good book. I am quite excited with the arguments that are raised.'

Although the book has taken some hits from blacks – Jeffrey Sammons, a history professor at New York University, called it 'racist' though he admitted he hadn't read it – the reaction from most African–Americans has been positive. The most hostile reaction has been from liberal whites. Anthropologist Jonathan Marks, in an opinion piece for the *New York Times*, called *Taboo* 'demagogic quackery' and a 'piece of good old-fashioned American anti–intellectualism'. Marks did not mention that he was criticised in the book for his neo-Creationist views and well-known political biases.

What are we to make of a phenomenon in which Establishment whites and blacks, so quick to crow about their own racial sensitivity, recklessly inject racial divisiveness into a debate in which scientists and most African–Americans see reason? The black community in particular has become irritated to the point of anger about the patronising censorship and codes of silence that many institutions employ to 'protect them'. 'I am an editorial columnist,' wrote Bill Maxwell of the *St Petersburg Times* in a note to me after his glowing column on *Taboo*. 'I reviewed your book because I enjoyed reading it. It cut through all of the bullshit. I am black.'

Humans are truly diverse, biologically and culturally. Acknowledging our differences may approach a danger zone, but pretending that there are no slippery questions does not prevent them from being asked, if only under one's breath. ❏

Jon Entine *is a writer and Emmy-winning producer for NBC and ABC News.* Taboo *is published by Public Affairs, US. More at www.jonentine.com*

JIM FIRSTLE

Temptation

Drugs are here to stay in world sport, but while the media hypes the big cases, officials look the other way and increasingly wealthy athletes buy themselves out of trouble

If you read the reams of copy put out every Olympic year about the 'War on Drugs' in sport, you might be tempted to believe that modern sport is infested with cheats and hypocrites. Woven into the typical pre-Olympic fluff are stories of athletes who will do anything to win a race, a competition, an Olympic gold medal. They are often aided by Frankenstein-like drug gurus and sporting officials who 'look the other way', ignoring the drug abuse in their midst.

While this may work in a Hollywood drama or for tabloid headlines, it ignores the fact that the use of drugs in sports reflects two basic human conditions: the lofty ideal embedded in the pursuit of excellence and the depths to which some will sink in the effort to be 'the best'. Over the years, physicians have purportedly conducted surveys among Olympic athletes using variants of the following question: 'If you could take a pill that would guarantee you a gold medal but would also lead to your premature death, would you take the pill?' The alleged result of the surveys was an overwhelming 'Yes!'

As Ben Johnson's coach, Charlie Francis, was fond of saying when he was asked why he used banned substances on his athletes: 'It isn't cheating if everybody else is doing it.' As the result of an under funded drug-testing system that doesn't even have tests for some of the substances that are banned, and a few high-profile drug busts, the notion that 'everybody's doing it' has been reinforced among many athletes and coaches. As long as that belief persists, it's hard for ambitious athletes to resist the temptation to take a pill or get an injection, particularly if they believe these aids will help them win an Olympic medal.

This fundamental truth is usually replaced in most sports coverage by the 'white hat, black hat' portrait of virtuous medal winners or disgraced drug cheats. There is no foolproof answer to the question 'How many athletes take drugs?' Testing does not catch everyone, and the nagging suspicion that this is so feeds rumours of grossly inflated figures of alleged doping among sport's elite, and the feeling that the person who set this world record or won that gold medal did so because he or she enlisted the help of the best pharmacist.

In the 1960s and 70s, sports officials tried to scare athletes by claiming that the drugs would kill them, that they would be caught and punished, that the drugs didn't work anyway. When such claims were exposed as fraudulent, distrust of sports officials, already pretty high, grew; the introduction of testing and the frequent proclamations by sports officials, such as International Olympic Committee chief Juan Antonio Samaranch, that the IOC was winning its War on Drugs had little credibility.

In the early years of drug testing, from 1964 to 1984, the IOC and member sporting federations lacked the money to develop a world-class drug-testing system. Nevertheless, they claimed their testing system 'worked' every time an athlete failed a doping test. But the athletic fraternity talked openly among itself about its drug taking and how to beat the tests. There is an old story, perhaps apocryphal, of the meeting of a gold and a silver medallist at the 1976 Olympics in Montreal. The gold medallist asks the silver medallist when, before the Games, he'd stopped taking anabolic steroids. When the silver medallist replied, the gold said, 'Oh, the same as me. We must be on the same programme.'

When the East German female swimmers showed up at the pool in Montreal with the shoulders of weightlifters, deep voices and world-record times, athletes from other countries knew the Germans were using something other than vitamins. Sports officials further damaged the credibility of their anti-doping programmes by noting that since these athletes had passed all their drug tests they must be 'clean'. The politics of international sport prevented the IOC, or any other organisation, from digging deeper into the GDR sports machine to uncover the dark secrets that were exposed when the Berlin Wall fell, and the state-controlled doping programme of GDR officials was revealed in the early 1990s.

Without proof, IOC and other sports officials claim, no action could be taken. But even after the 1984 Olympics in Los Angeles had turned the Games into a financial bonanza for the IOC, no well-funded research and development project was launched to fight the sports world's largely rhetorical 'War on Drugs'. Those who were monitoring the doping phenomenon, such as Penn State University epidemiologist Chuck Yesalis, continued to insist that athletes using drugs were always one step ahead of those doing the testing. Dr Don Catlin, who runs the IOC accredited drug-testing laboratory in Los Angeles, likened the situation to attempts between the Cold War superpowers to negotiate nuclear non-proliferation treaties. One side would only crack down and get tough on its drug cheats if the other country did the same. To bust one's drug cheats without the gesture being reciprocated put the anti-doping nation at a competitive disadvantage.

US athletes believed their competitors used drugs. The Soviets, East Germans and other rivals of the US for sporting supremacy believed the US was more riddled with drug-enhanced athletes than any other country in the world. Hadn't a US doctor, John Ziegler, invented anabolic steroids? Yes, as a response to the discovery in 1956 that the Soviet weightlifters were injecting themselves with testosterone. Back and forth it went, creating an escalating atmosphere of suspicion and clandestine doping. Instead of saying don't take drugs, the ethos seemed to be don't get caught.

As technology made more substances available, the job of drug testing became more demanding. But spending on research into detecting and testing of doping agents remained negligible. Meanwhile, Olympic sports became more professional with the open payment of prize and endorsement money. Athletes became wealthy. When banned substances were detected in their urine, they could hire expert witnesses or lawyers to argue that the tests themselves were flawed. The lack of proper research and development funding for the Olympic drug-testing system was exposed as appeals panels overturned doping cases against athletes and doubts were raised on the veracity of some testing methods. At the 1996 Olympics in Atlanta, the results of tests detecting the use of a banned substance, Bromantan, were overturned on appeal to the Court for Arbitration for Sport because of an inadequate defence and poorly written doping legislation.

Sporting federations, it seemed, could not catch and convict those labelled as drug cheats. In 1998, media coverage turned the World

Swimming Championships into the 'doping games' after Australian customs agents discovered synthetic human growth hormone in the luggage of Chinese swimmers. The substance had been banned by the IOC even though there was no test that could detect its use. Later that year, the Tour de France was similarly besieged when French customs agents caught an employee of Team Festina attempting to deliver a car full of banned substances to his team.

Again in 1998, Irish swimmer Michelle de Bruin, who has always insisted she had not taken drugs when she won several gold medals at the 1996 Olympics, was convicted by the world swimming federation of attempting to hide the fact that she might have had banned drugs in her urine. A US major league baseball player, Mark McGwire, was caught taking an anabolic steroid precursor, Androstenedione. The substance was not banned by baseball and his record-breaking home-run totals helped send sales of 'Andro' through the roof. Beset by all these scandals, Samaranch called for an emergency meeting on doping in sport. After the meeting, the IOC committed US$25 million to the formation of a new worldwide anti-doping agency.

Throughout the scandals and alarms, the focus of attention was always on the battle between the 'drug cheats' and those trying to catch them; the tabloid-style coverage made no serious attempt to discover why sports was beset by this problem. Drug use was there before money and technology became major players. Those who are convicted of doping offences are branded cheats and discarded like used sporting equipment. But is Mark McGwire really all that different from Michelle de Bruin? Both share the same skills, the same ambitions, the same temptations; but one benefits from different rules. If the governing bodies of sports make rules banning certain substances, they must, at least, allocate the funds necessary to ensure they have the best scientifically developed and judicially approved tests.

Is the media, too, shirking its duty by plastering headlines about every athlete that flunks a drug test over the front pages, while not aggressively investigating the shortcomings of the testing system used to convict the athletes? A drug-testing system that hides the results of its tests on the grounds of protecting athletes also protects the guilty. But editors don't want dreary stories about the mechanics of the drug-testing process; the sports pages are a place where readers go to discover the uplifting side of human nature, they say. Meanwhile, every elite athlete who aspires to get

Ben Johnson winning the Olympic 100m at Seoul. He was later stripped of his medal after a failed drugs test – Credit: Tony Duffy/Allsports

to the top has to answer one simple question: 'What am I willing to do to get there?' ❏

Jim Firstle is a freelance writer based in St. Paul, Minnesota, USA. His work on drugs in sport has appeared on the BBC and CBS's 60 Minutes, in the New York Times, *the* Sunday Times, Runner's World Daily *and* Athletics Weekly

FA'EZEH HASHEMI

Flying the chador

'How do you do your karate training in Afghanistan,' I asked her. 'You must be joking,' she replied. 'If they knew I was doing karate, they'd slice off my head and put it into my hands.' It's not always easy for women in the Muslim world to indulge a passion for sport. But with two Islamic Women's Games behind them, Iran is beginning to change male attitudes

'Muslim women, too, want to have an arena; they want to be motivated. It's their right to be able to practise their sport at championship level. We have two Islamic Women's Games behind us: the first Games with the participation of ten Islamic countries and, this time [1998], with 24. Islamic countries in general are not very advanced in sports, but the relatively low standard must not deter us from organising competitions.

'We have problems with Arab countries: they find it difficult to allow girls to travel on their own, without their parents, as members of sports teams. Nevertheless, I'm pleased with the results. The number of sports clubs has increased in Bahrain and in Oman. Kuwait, too, since it established contact with us, has set up several state-owned sports clubs. And, last year, they appointed a woman to take charge of women's sports. I'm sure the situation of women from Arab countries will have improved by the next Games.

'Islamic countries can be divided into two groups: one group consists of countries in which – like our own country before the revolution – a percentage of women are excluded from taking part in sports because they want to observe Islamic criteria. We want these countries to understand that they, too, have a duty to organise Islamic sports. The fact that these competitions were covered by the foreign media let women in other countries know what was happening. For example, British Muslim women wrote to us asking to be allowed to participate in the next Games. The second group includes countries such as Bahrain, Kuwait, Oman, and so on, which have simply put women's sports to one side. When we organise competitions, they realise that it is possible to participate in sports while observing all Islamic criteria. We are laying cultural foundations, and that could take ten years or more.

'It would be good if, as an international movement, we were able to hold these Games in different countries. But we can't sacrifice Islamic criteria to achieve this. Indonesia and Malaysia have volunteered to hold the next Games. We'll have to see whether they can adhere to Islamic conditions or not. If they can't, there'd be nothing wrong with holding the next few Games in Iran. Iranian women want competition. They want sports. Yes, we have shortcomings. But you mustn't forget that competition itself motivates sports people. But if we didn't even hold these Games, how would some girl in Sirjan, for example, learn that sport is on the increase in this country?

'The [Iranian] papers hardly bothered to report these Games. Still, I was satisfied by their effort; radio and television also performed better than in previous years. Because they were afraid that women's sports might suffer [as a result of media coverage], radio and television had ignored the problem altogether for a long time: ignored half the population. Their excuse was that they couldn't cover women's sports visually. They still haven't found a solution to this 19 years after [the Revolution]. They prefer to play politics.

'But the foreign media were interested and, on the whole, the Games were held in a very respectable manner. Under the banner of sports, we were able to undo the negative propaganda directed against Muslim women and, especially, Iranian women. Nothing has ever given us the positive publicity this did ... We should leave politics out of it and get on with the practical side of things.' ❑

Fa'ezeh Hashemi *is the head of the Islamic Countries' Women's Sports Solidarity Council and founding editor of* Zan. *This interview first appeared in* Zanan *which is currently banned*
Translated by Nilou Mobasser

SIMON MARTIN

Modern Mussolinis

There's nothing new in the use of sport to build nations, glorify leaders and pursue war by other means. Mussolini went into it big time in the 1930s; Serbs and Croats are still at it today

When the Yugoslav footballer Zoran Mirkovic grabbed the testicles of his Croatian adversary, Robert Jarni, during the highly charged Euro 2000 qualification match last year in Zagreb, it was not the act of another petulant, overpaid, self-inflated soccer star, but a twist for a nation scorned. Sent off for his troubles, Mirkovic waved goodbye to the Croatian crowd with a three-fingered Serbian salute. Although Croatia failed to achieve the necessary victory to reach this summer's finals in Holland and Belgium, the legion of war-wounded wheeled in to accompany the huge 'Vukovar 91' banner at the pitch side ensured that nobody forgot or mistook the real issues at stake. Indeed, prior to the disintegration of Yugoslavia regular outbreaks of fan violence had anticipated the impending war to come.

During the more recent conflict in Kosovo, many Yugoslav footballers chose to use their fame and status to campaign against the NATO air strikes, such as the Lazio defender Sinisa Mihajlovic who sported a T-shirt emblazoned with the message 'Peace not War'. Following the murder of 'Arkan', in January this year, Mihajlovic forgot his pacifist leanings and published an obituary in a Belgrade newspaper in praise of the indicted war criminal. His faux pas was swiftly followed by the Lazio ultras' (unofficial fan group) own touching tribute in a banner unfurled at the Olympic Stadium, proclaiming 'Honour to the Tiger Arkan'.

In response, the Italian government imposed rapid legal measures intended to combat the recent increase in extremism on the terraces, and all clubs became legally responsible for the actions of their fans and accountable for any future indiscretions. This relationship between football (*calcio*) and politics is long-term, particularly in the Italian peninsula, where it was first exploited by the Fascist government.

In 1934, Italy hosted and won the World Cup, the tournament providing a perfect international propaganda opportunity for the Fascist regime. Sixteen teams competed across eight Italian cities to the accompaniment of a strong Fascist presence at all matches, with Benito Mussolini personally attending all Italian fixtures. This success was swiftly followed by victory in the 1936 Olympic soccer competition and retention of the World Cup in 1938. With Europe on the brink of war, this victory in France was arguably even more important for the regime, so much so that that on the eve of the final Mussolini sent the team a personal telegram with the simple message 'Win or Die'!

The Fascist politicisation of *calcio* gave it a symbolic dimension, which often exposed teams to political opposition. As the regime became more extreme so the protests intensified, to the point where, on arrival in Marseilles at the start of the 1938 World Cup, the national team train was attacked by thousands of anti-Fascists and exiled Italians. Such was Mussolini's displeasure at this lack of hospitality, he ordered the team's 'away' colours be changed from the traditional white to a provocative black.

Despite the intention to manufacture consent and forge a unified Italian national identity, *calcio* frequently exposed the contradictions and cleavages within Italian Fascist society, such as the star status conferred on certain players, which exposed the conflict between public and private duty. The striker Giuseppe Meazza, who could justifiably be considered the David Beckham of his era were it not for his cross-national appeal and superior appreciation of the concept of style, was adored both on and off the field of play by men and women alike. An integral and focal part of the Italian team, he portrayed a positive image of Italy and the 'New Fascist man', but his off-the-field leisure pursuits, which included gambling and serial monogamy, rendered his role model status less than satisfactory. The regime was unable to disguise the fact that its attempt had, on occasion, met serious resistance but, most significantly, the Fascist government had set the example for others to follow.

In 1976, some members of the new military regime in Argentina felt the country could not afford to stage the already designated 1978 World

World Cup, 1934. The Italian team raise their arms in fascist salute before playing Czechoslovakia – Credit: Hulton Deutsch

Cup. Despite their reservations, the allocation of some ten per cent of the national budget for 1978 saw the nation ready. Domestically, the population was bombarded with patriotic slogans, as once again companies placed television sets in factories and offices, and families were encouraged to alter their daily routines according to the fixtures.

Meanwhile, less desirable citizens 'disappeared'. Allegations of government interference and corruption to ensure the 'correct' result further echoed the 1930s. Recounting Argentina's improbable 6-0 victory over Peru to secure a place in the final, Tony Mason says: '[O]nly the Brazilians and Alemann, the Minister of the Interior who had been critical of the cost were suspicious. The Brazilians, because FIFA had foolishly allowed their game with Poland to be played before Argentina met Peru, which meant, as Argentina and Brazil would have equal points if both won, that Argentina would know exactly how many goals were required to win their place in the final. Alemann, because a bomb exploded at his home at the precise moment when the all-important fourth goal was scored.'

Four years later, football shared the airwaves with the official coverage of the Malvinas war as matches became conduits for the recreation of the national euphoria of 1978.

In 1986, with the physical and mental wounds still fresh, Diego Maradona single-handedly restored the nation's pride with a display of genius and guile, scoring twice in the 2-1 victory over England in the World Cup quarter-final. His second strike, the culmination of a run of more than half the length of the pitch in which he committed the serial humiliation of one English player after another, effectively won the tie. However, it was Maradona's first – via either his hand, or that of 'God' – that brought the nation catharsis, as he illegally punched the ball into the net. After the match the Argentine manager Cesar Luis Menotti described the importance of the 'goal': 'Now we've had the good fortune not only that Maradona has been admired everywhere in the world, but that he scored that goal, precisely against the English, just four years after the Malvinas war. He scores that goal with his hand. "Better yet!" people say. "In the war, OK, we lost, but at football we busted their arse with a goal scored with a handball."'

In that split second, as much as was humanly possible, Maradona avenged the wounded pride of a nation. Soon after, he repeated the feat, but this time on behalf of Italy's downtrodden Neapolitans, when, in 1987 and 1990, he led Napoli to the only two *scudetti* (Italian championships) in its history, poking 'one in the eye' of all the northern clubs – and their fans – that felt a divine right to dominate football, economics and politics.

In many countries, it is once again advantageous to be seen as a 'football person' when seeking to establish and maintain political office. British politics recently witnessed, with varying degrees of authenticity, the emergence from the closet of a number of celebrity MP 'supporters', such as David Mellor and Tony Banks, while in Italy, prior to his election as prime minster, Silvio Berlusconi regularly spoke in terms of taking his squad into the field of play. Although already a major public figure in Italy through his media empire, prior to bankrolling AC Milan, Berlusconi's involvement in football expanded his opportunities for political involvement and self-aggrandisement. Take this scenario to the extreme, and we return to the career of Arkan. Built on the back of football alongside his mafia activities, by the time he died he owned the Yugoslav club Obilic. More sinister was his earlier control of the youth brigades of Red Star Belgrade's supporters' association. Having contributed to the precipitation of the Yugoslav conflict on the terraces, his loyal supporters formed the core of the Serbian Volunteer Guard or 'Tigers' that raped, murdered and plundered as the vanguard of Yugoslav forces in Bosnia.

Unquestionably, political regimes have been guilty of politicising and manipulating football, but it is arguable that they were less irresponsible in the use of their power and influence than today's brokers. Governments' financial investments in the game could only ever buy breathing space, as even World Cup victories cannot solve economic, political and social problems. As football fast approaches implosion it remains to be seen whether FIFA can responsibly determine its future or whether the ball has already been passed to the Mussolinis of our age. ❏

Simon Martin is an FA-qualified football coach currently conducting PhD research into football, Fascism and Italian identity in Mussolini's Italy

SIMON KUPER

Cheering the enemy

In many dictatorships, dissent through football may be the only form of protest available. Thus it was with Herr Klopfleisch...

Helmut Klopfleisch is one of the German football fans you won't be reading about in this month's tabloids. He's not a neo-Nazi. He has never fought at a match. He has, however, been tailed by the secret police and arrested several times for being a football fan. Klopfleisch used to be a football dissident. Over the last few decades there have been thousands, perhaps millions, like him.

I met Klopfleisch in Berlin nearly a decade ago. He is a large, moon-faced man who in mid-1989 was expelled from the GDR to West Germany. I became his biographer, and to make my task easier, he sent me photocopies from the files that the Stasi, the East German secret police, kept on him. It is a tribute to the Stasi that its account of his life tallies almost entirely with his own.

Klopfleisch, both sources agree, was born in East Berlin in 1948. He worked as an electrician in a People's Company, and later as a window cleaner in a rare private firm. He likes to talk or, as the Stasi puts it, he has 'an emotional manner founded in his character'. The file warns: 'K has a good mental grasp and is able to recognise connections.' (Had the *Stasi* not used his initial, the file would read a little less like Kafka.) On politics, the file says: 'In K's opinion sport and politics have nothing to do with one another.'

This was not a view the Stasi shared. When the western bureaucrat handed Klopfleisch his file, she told him: 'It's all about football!'

'K calls himself a fanatical supporter of the West Berlin football club Hertha BSC,' the file says. As a child, he used to walk from East Berlin to West to see Hertha play at home. After the Berlin Wall went up, on

13 August 1961, he spent a few Saturday afternoons standing beside it among a horde of eastern Hertha fans listening to the sounds from the club's ground a few hundred yards away on the western side. The border guards soon put a stop to that.

Later, Klopfleisch helped found an illegal 'Hertha Society', which would meet once a month to talk about their club. Often the Hertha manager would cross from West Berlin to visit them, but the Stasi grew suspicious, and would try to stop the manager at the border.

Klopfleisch told me: 'I supported Hertha, Bayern Munich and the West German national team, but really I used to back any western club against any eastern side. I was there when Dynamo Berlin played Aston Villa, when they played Liverpool, when Vorwärts Frankfurt played Manchester United. I love Manchester United. I remember a Denis Law header from 20 yards out that was like another player's shot.'

In three decades, Klopfleisch saw Hertha play once, in Poland, against Lech Poznan. There was a great queue at the Polish border that day, but the German border guards knew about the match and were turning people back. Klopfleisch had anticipated this. He had brought his mother along. At the frontier he pointed at her and said, 'She grew up in Poland. I'm taking her to see her old home.' The border guards let him through and he saw Hertha play. However, the Stasi knew about the trip. It appears in their catalogue of his football journeys abroad.

The Stasi, sparing no expense, accompanied him everywhere. 'K, by his behaviour at the People's Republic of Bulgaria v the Federal Republic of Germany, has significantly damaged the international reputation of the GDR,' an agent reported sadly. It mentions a number of other football dissidents who had likewise blotted the GDR's noble reputation.

When Bayern Munich visited Czechoslovakia in 1981, the Stasi took measures 'to prevent the arrival of inimical negative forces/criminally dangerous persons, as also negative decadent young people and youths.' It failed. Klopfleisch's file reports: '... a large number of football fans, in large part citizens of the GDR, assembled in front of [Bayern's] hotel ... To restore order and safety, the Czech militia was compelled to clear the hotel entrance, through the use of truncheons, among other methods. The action of the militia ... was filmed from the window of a hotel room by a male person using a cine-film camera.' It was Klopfleisch.

In December 1981, Lieutenant Hoyer of the Stasi summoned

Klopfleisch for a meeting. Hoyer suggested that in future he let the Stasi know if he planned to watch a western team. Klopfleisch began to sulk. 'This did not appeal to him at all,' the file reports, 'he stated that in that case he would lose all pleasure and interest in the match. He already had the impression of being under control.'

Klopfleisch was repeatedly interrogated after that. 'They always wanted to know who else was in it with me,' he says. 'I made a point of never giving them any names.' The file remarks: 'K possesses a politically labile stance.'

He continued to watch western teams all over the Iron Curtain, continued to be arrested and, in 1989, as his mother lay on her deathbed, was expelled with his wife and son to West Germany. His mother died a few days later. He was not allowed back for her funeral.

Klopfleisch's tale is bizarre, but hardly unique. His own Stasi file mentions large numbers of 'football dissidents' who lived much the same life as he did. Each time West Germany won the World Cup – in 1954, 1974 and 1990 – there were private celebrations, sometimes with fireworks, all over the GDR. The only time the GDR and West Germany met, at that World Cup of 1974, the East Germans won 1-0 thanks to a Jurgen Sparwasser goal. Sparwasser, who later defected to West Germany, claims that his fellow East Germans always made him feel guilty for having scored. Klopfleisch says of that game: 'It was a day of mourning in our house.'

Football dissidence can be defined as follows: expressing dissent against a regime by supporting football teams that play against the regime's team. Often, in a dictatorship, football dissidence is the only available form of mass dissent. In a football stadium, 80,000 people can gather and shout more or less what they like. It is easy to arrest the writer of a naughty article in a *samizdat* publication; harder to shut up a football crowd, which in any case has a louder voice. Furthermore, the stadium offers anonymity. Ho Chi Minh illicitly founded the Vietnamese Communist Party in a Hong Kong stadium during a football match.

The regime's team opposed by football dissidents is often the national side: the GDR, say, or the Soviet Union. It can also be a club sponsored by the regime. All teams in eastern Europe named Dynamo were funded by the Interior Ministry. Dynamo Berlin, for instance, played in their latter years under the presidency of Stasi chief Erich Mielke. Mielke,

WAR BY OTHER MEANS

'Sport is war minus the shooting.'
George Orwell

1972'S WORLD CHESS CHAMPIONSHIP between America's Bobby Fischer and Russia's Boris Spassky, was played at the height of the Cold War and became symbolic of that struggle. Fischer was the first non-Russian since 1948 to challenge for the championship which was played in Reykjavik in the full glare of the media. After much politicking – including a call from US Secretary of State Henry Kissinger urging Fischer not to give in – and Russian accusations of 'mind control devices' planted by the US, Fischer eventually won, breaking 24 years of Soviet domination.

THE 1936 OLYMPICS IN BERLIN planned as Hitler's showcase for Aryan superiority, were dominated by a black US athlete, Jesse Owens. He won four gold medals, setting two world records in the process. A year earlier, Owens set five world records in 45 minutes, becoming one of the greatest sportsmen ever. President Roosevelt neither invited Owens to the White House nor sent him a letter congratulating him on his achievements.

THE MEXICO OLYMPICS OF 1968 were played against the backdrop of global political unrest and the Vietnam War. Black US athletes competing in the tournament displayed solidarity with the civil rights/black power movements by making their own protests during the games. The most memorable of these was the protest by Tommie Smith and John Carlos, gold and bronze medal winners of the 200 metres. Both wore black scarves around their necks to symbolise lynchings endured by blacks in the South, and black gloves on fists raised in the black power salute. Neither ever represented their countries again (*Index* 6/1999).

IN MOSCOW 1980 AND LOS ANGELES 1984, the USA and the Soviet Union mutually boycotted each other's Olympics. Cold War tension was running high, with proxy foreign wars being fought in Nicaragua fghanistan and Angola, to name nly a few. Direct sporting onfrontations with the inevitable efeat of one or t'other was voided; but East German women, ow known to have been pumped ull of performance-enhancing eroids, dominated their events.

HE TERM 'NUCLEAR CRICKET' was oined in 1988 when Pakistan and dia, each with recent nuclear tests nder their belt and continuing onfrontation in Kashmir, let their ostility spill over onto the cricket itch in the 1999 test series.

T THE 1994 FOOTBALL WORLD CUP an beat USA 1-0. In Iran, the victory as followed by huge celebrations. eople danced and sang in the eets, ecstatic at having defeated e 'Great Satan' which had pposed the Revolution implacably r 15 years.

UBA'S BASEBALL VICTORY over the USA the 1996 Olympic baseball final in anta was a triumphant moment for Castro's Cuba, for over 40 years the victim of US-imposed sanctions.

'I AIN'T GOT NO QUARREL WITH THEM VIET CONG,' said heavyweight boxer Muhammed Ali, on refusing to report for the draft in 1966. As a result he was stripped of his title on 23 March 1967, a decision that was overturned by the Supreme Court in 1970. Ali regained his title in 1974, knocking out George Foreman.

CROAT AND SERB FANS fought during a football match between Red Star Belgrade (Serbia) and Dynamo Zagreb (Croatia) in Croatia in 1990, a portent of the war to come scarcely a year later. Serb police reacted harshly with their violence directed mainly at the Croats. A Croat player, Zvonimir Boban, attacked the police with a karate-style kick. The Yugoslav football authorities suspended Boban from the national team; to Croatia he became a folk hero. ❏

Compiled by Tony Callaghan and Humfrey Hunter

who died last month, forced all good GDR players to join his club, leaned on referees, and helped Dynamo win the East German title every year from 1979 to 1988.

Known as 'The Eleven Pigs', Dynamo were not very popular. To oppose them was to oppose the regime. It was similar all over the Eastern bloc. Anecdotal evidence suggests that at a Dynamo Moscow game in 1937, at the height of Stalin's purges, the crowd at a Dynamo game suddenly began whistling and sustained this for several minutes as one man. Nowhere else in the Soviet Union in 1937 could a crowd express its dissent.

So strong was football dissidence in eastern Europe that for many people it seems to have been the main motive for watching matches. It is noteworthy that in Albania, the most repressive state in Communist Europe, football attendance per head of population was the highest in Europe in the 1980s. In Soviet republics like Armenia and Lithuania, local fans regarded their football team as an emblem of their nation. This feeling was particularly potent during the Gorbachev era, when the USSR began to disintegrate. Each time Yerevan Ararat, the Armenian side, beat a team from Moscow, Armenians would march through the town chanting 'Ararat' – the name of the team, but also of a mountain in Turkey claimed by Armenians and hence a nationalist symbol.

In Lithuania, fans of Zalgiris Vilnius would march into town after matches carrying torches and singing folk songs, and would be met by militiamen with batons – 'bananas', as the Lithuanians called them. Andrius Kubilius, who this spring became Lithuania's prime minister, told me in 1992 that football and basketball had been 'vital' in the struggle for independence.

When freedom came, eastern Europeans stopped going to football. In part this was because the best players moved West – virtually the whole Dynamo Berlin side emigrated. But it was also because football lost much of its significance. Klopfleisch, who has spent the last decade in West Berlin, still watches Hertha and follows Germany abroad, often spending nights sleeping in his car, although his health has declined. He will watch at least one German game at Euro 2000. But he tells me that football means less to him than it used to. Watching Germany win Euro '96 had been pleasant. When he lived in the GDR, it was more important than that.

The rule of thumb is that the more repressive the regime, the more important is football dissidence. The most significant appearance of the phenomenon in recent years occurred, therefore, in Libya. Reports differ as to exactly what happened. However, it seems that at a game in Tripoli on 9 July 1996, the referee allowed a contentious goal scored by the team run by Colonel Ghaddafi's son Saidi. The crowd began chanting anti-Ghaddafi slogans, whereupon Saidi, his brother Muhammad and their bodyguards apparently opened fire. The spectators stampeded out of the ground onto the streets, where they stoned cars and continued chanting their slogans. (An alternative interpretation is that some of the shooting was between Saidi's and Muhammad's rival camps.)

The US department of state says that to its knowledge this riot was 'the last display of public discontent and resentment towards the government'. No wonder, since in Libya 'public assembly is permitted only with regime approval and in support of the regime's positions'. In other words, only at a football match can a Libyan crowd register dissent.

Accounts of similar football riots have emerged in recent years from Iraq. They have quite likely also happened in Burma and other highly repressive states. Often it is impossible to know for sure. Such riots are not reported in local newspapers. What is clear is that we must be aware as football as a source of free expression in dictatorial states, alongside illegal publications, Internet sites, church services, and so on. ❏

Simon Kuper is a columnist with the London Observer *and the author of* Football against the Enemy *(Orion). This article is based on a talk given to the Cold War Cultures and Society workshop at Warwick University in March. For more information on the workshop, an ongoing project dealing with the cultural history of the Cold War, contact Patrick Major at P.N.Major@warwick.ac.uk*

INDEX INDEX

Weep for Assad? 'Not bloody likely!'

'The great leader lives and can never die.' 'O miracle of our age! You led us in your absence as well as in our midst and lead us still in death'. Even allowing for the natural rhetoric of the language, the headlines in the Syrian press that bade farewell to Hafez Assad, set new standards in funereal panegyric.

As did the roll-call of achievement: for instance, the editorial pages of *Al Wahda* (Unity) revealed that the great leader's selfless and tireless promotion of the rights of women had 'spared our Syrian women the cries and lamentations of western women forced to descend into the streets to fight for their rights…'.

Maybe that was only to be expected from a media that is about as liberated and even handed as *Pravda*. But our own dear media? By and large, the western press held its tongue: comment by omission. Not a word about the thousands that languish in Syrian jails merely for suggesting there might be another way of doing things; or the omnipresent *muhabarat* and other even more secret services that render Syria a state of fear; the waterwheels that ran red with blood in Homs – where the ruins of a razed city are preserved to strike fear into its citizens – or Hama where up to 20,000 were killed over three months in 1982 to destroy the challenge of the Muslim Brothers once and for all.

No. Assad brought stability to Syria after years of internecine feuding, and he was pivotal in the pursuit of peace in the Middle East. But at what price? There is a roll-call of a different kind.

Numan Ali Abdu: Journalist with the Lebanese weekly *Al-Tarik*, arrested in 1992 and sentenced to 15 years. Held in the notorious military prison of Tadmor, scene in the 1980s of mass public executions conducted by another Assad – Rifaat, troublesome brother to Hafez.

Faysal Allush: Poet and journalist arrested on suspicion of membership in the Party for Communist Action in 1992. Sentenced to 15 years; held incommunicado for seven.

Faraj Ahmad Bayrakdar: Poet and journalist arrested in 1987 on suspicion of membership of the PCA. Tried by military court after five years detention and sentenced to 15 years. Held incommunicado for seven. Injured by torture and cannot walk unaided.

Samir al-Hassan: Palestinian journalist and editor with *al-Qaida* and *Fatah al-Intififada*. Arrested in 1986 accused of membership of PCA; tried after eight years detention and sentenced to 15 years. Held in Tadmor.

Aslan Abdelkarim: Teacher and editor-in-chief of two underground magazines linked to the CPA, *Al Nida Al Chabi* and *Al Raya Al Amra*, both banned in 1992. Arrested in 1984 and sentenced to 15 years.

Adel Ismael: Said to have been detained since 1996 on grounds that he was a militant member of the banned Democratic Bass Party.

Marwan Mohamad: Journalist with weekly *Al-Baath* arrested in 1987 and sentenced to ten years in 1993.

And the good news: **Salama George Kayla**, writer and journalist arrested in 1992 and sentenced to eight years for peaceful opposition and his newspaper writing, was reportedly released on 21 March 2000.

All suffer the marks of torture; many are seriously ill as a result of a lack of medical care. Many have been awarded journalism's most prestigious prizes while in prison, including **Nizar Nayyuf,** winner in June of the 2000 Golden Pen of Freedom awarded by the World Association of Newspapers. In a message smuggled out of Al Mezze in April, Nayyuf describes the prison as 'one of the most savage, bloody, criminal and secretive places in the world. Between three and five people die from torture every day ... this cemetery of living creatures.'

Nayyuf was arrested in 1992 and sentenced to ten years hard labour and 'deprivation of political rights' for 'disseminating false information' via *Sawt al-Democratiyya*, the newsletter of the banned Committee for the Defence of Democratic Freedoms and Human Rights, of which he was editor-in-chief. A 'confession' was extorted under torture and he is now unable to walk without a stick. He also suffers from cancer and is said to be in urgent need of treatment.

The writers and journalists are only a fraction of those incarcerated in Assad's prisons, frequently without trial and often for little more than the expression of an opinion.

And so, finally, to the last question: for what? The biggest army in the region; a central role for Syria in regional politics and the protection of what Damascus calls its 'soft underbelly' with the occupation of Lebanon. The cost of which has left Syria bankrupt, kept afloat only by the hyperactive black market; a sullen, impoverished and resentful populace – particularly in the countryside; a culture that was once the pride of the Arab world, stifled, its poets in exile or prison; all debate, social as well as political, stifled; no foreseeable way forward into another century; the 'stability' by which the West set such store in danger of collapse; and that 'peace' in the middle east – in the cause of which Hafez Assad was given such an easy ride to the grave – even further off. ❏

Judith Vidal Hall

A censorship chronicle incorporating information from the American Association for the Advancement of Science Human Rights Action Network (AAASHRAN), Amnesty International (AI), Article 19 (A19), Alliance of Independent Journalists (AJI), the BBC Monitoring Service Summary of World Broadcasts (SWB), the Committee to Protect Journalists (CPJ), Canadian Journalists for Free Expression (CJFE), Glasnost Defence Foundation (GDF), Instituto de Prensa y Sociedad (IPYS), The UN's Integrated Regional Information Network (IRIN), the Inter-American Press Association (IAPA), the International Federation of Journalists (IFJ/FIP), Human Rights Watch (HRW), the Media Institute of Southern Africa (MISA), Network for the Defence of Independent Media in Africa (NDIMA), International PEN (PEN), Open Media Research Institute (OMRI), Pacific Islands News Association (PINA), Radio Free Europe/Radio Liberty (RFE/RL), Reporters Sans Frontières (RSF), the World Association of Community Broadcasters (AMARC), World Association of Newspapers (WAN), the World Organisation Against Torture (OMCT) and other sources

ANGOLA

Journalist **Andres Domingos Mussamo** was found not guilty of violating state secrets, it was reported on 6 June (*Index* 2/2000, 3/2000). He had been charged with 'stealing state documents and violating state secrets'. (MISA)

ARGENTINA

Media coverage of the inhumane living conditions found in a children's home run by the Catholic Church provoked the wrath of several clergymen. The Archbishop of Mercedes-Luján, Emilio Ogñenovich, who had jurisdiction over the home, hurled insults at journalist **María Julia Oliván** of TV programme *Día D* and *XXII* magazine when she tried to question him after mass on 29 April. On 17 May Rev Julio Forchi of the same diocese wrote in his regular column in daily *El Oeste* that journalists 'should undergo a lobotomy to see if that will help them calm down'. In another outburst, the Bishop of Lomas de Zamora, Desiderio Collino, told churchgoers on 21 May that journalists who criticise the Catholic Church 'deserve to contract lung cancer'. (Periodistas)

An edition of the political review *3 Puntos* was given the equivalent of an X certificate on 11 May by the censorship body, Comisión Calificadora de Espectáculos, Publicaciones y Expresiones Gráficas, for publishing sexually explicit works by well-known artists in its inside pages. However, the censors were forced to backtrack after editor **Jorge Halperín** successfully appealed to the secretary of culture and the head of Buenos Aires' municipal government. (Periodistas)

ARMENIA

The Moscow radio station Mayak, closed in September 1996 by then president Levon Ter-Petrosian, resumed broadcasting in Armenia in mid-May. The station plans to operate 24 hours a day, seven days a week, with a mix of Mayak and Armenian material. (Snark, RFE/RL)

Vahagn Ghukasian, a contributor to the Yerevan-based daily *Aravot*, the daily *Haykakan Jamanak* and the weekly *Chorrord Ishkhanutiun*, was taken on 6 June to the Interior Ministry where two senior officers interrogated and beat him severely. Ghukasian believes he was attacked in retaliation for a 20-page brochure entitled *An Observer's Version*, which was published on 27 May and disseminated to journalists and politicians. The brochure reported on the investigation into the 27 October 1999 attack on Parliament. (CPJ)

AUSTRIA

Professor Anton Pelinka of Innsbruck University was found guilty on 23 May of defaming Jorg Haider, who stepped down as leader of the Freedom Party on 1 May. The political scientist was fined Asch60,000 (US$4,500) for saying in an interview with Italy's RAI TV that 'Haider has repeatedly made statements which amount to trivialising National Socialism. Once he described death camps as penal camps.' Haider's lawyer, Dieter Bohmdorfer, who initiated the proceedings against Pelinka in May 1999, is now the minister of justice. (International Helsinki Federation for Human Rights)

AZERBAIJAN

Reporters called on 18 April for

the release of their colleague **Vardan Taschian**, who has been arrested by Armenian authorities in the disputed enclave of Nagorno-Karabagh in the wake of the 22 March attempted assassination of Karabagh President Arkady Ghukasian. Taschian had been working in Karabagh since 1990, first as a contributor to *Azat Artstakh* daily, then as director of a news service and, since 1999, for the *Tasnerod Nahang* local weekly. (Armenpress, RFE/RL)

Opposition journalist **Vahram Aghajanian** was released from jail in Nagorno-Karabagh on 27 April after an appeals court suspended his one-year sentence for slandering Prime Minister Anushavan Danielian in an article last November (*Index* 3/2000). (RFE/RL)

Seventeen journalists were beaten and at least one arrested at an unsanctioned 29 April opposition rally in Baku. The 17 included five from *Bu Gun* newspaper and others from *Yeni Musavat*, *525-ci Gazet*, *Eliller*, *Gunaydin*, *Avropa*, *Hurriyyet*, *Elchi* and *Reytinq*. *Intibakh* journalist **Vagif Hajibeyli** remained in custody until 8 May, when the Yeni Nesil Journalists' Union issued a statement expressing concern over his deteriorating health. (Azerbaijan Journalists' Trade Union, CPJ, RFE/RL)

The Economic Court on 16 May suspended publication of *Monitor Weekly* and froze its assets. Tax officials accused editor **Elmar Huseinov**, who also edits the opposition newspaper *Bakinski Bulvar*, of failing to present

financial data for the first three months of the year. On 31 May Huseinov and *Bakinski Bulvar* journalist **Irada Huseinova** were fined ten million manats (US$2,270) each for an article allegedly insulting Defence Minister Safar Abiev by implicating him in 'economic crime'. Huseinov told Turan news agency on 13 June that, prompted by official harassment, he intends to approach a western embassy in Baku to request political asylum. *Monitor Weekly*'s predecessor, *Monitor*, ceased publication in mid-1998 after a Baku court fined it for insulting senior officials (*Index* 3/1998, 4/1998). (Azerbaijan Journalists' Trade Union, RFE/RL, AP, Interfax, Turan)

On 27 May 15 to 20 police attacked the offices of *Bu Gun* newspaper after two of its staff, journalist **Revan Chinghizoglu** and photographer **Eldeniz Bedelsoy**, were sent to report on a fracas between police and high-school students celebrating their graduation. The two men showed their press cards but the police began to insult and beat Chinghizoglu. Bedlesoy photographed the beating and, when noticed, ran back to the newspaper's office. A group of police followed Bedelsoy and attacked the newspaper's offices, beating any journalist who questioned what they were doing. Finally, they took Bedelsoy to the police station. The two were only released after editor-in-chief **Nesib Ismayilov** demanded an explanation. (Azerbaijan Journalists' Trade Union)

On 30 May a Baku court found

the newspaper *Uch Nogte* guilty of 'insulting the honour and dignity' of Astara District Administrator Ibragim Guliev. (Turan)

Representatives of 95 staff from Sara Radio and Television reported in early June that despite eight months of attempts to appeal against the closure of the station (*Index* 6/1999, 1/2000, 2/2000, 3/2000) they had not yet secured a court date. (Sara TV)

BANGLADESH

On 29 April **Muniruzzaman Monir**, correspondent for the daily *Prothom Alo* of Rupgonj, was beaten by leaders of the ruling Awami League's student wing because of a story he had written. Local police refuse to hear Monir's complaint because he 'belongs to the governing party'. (Media Watch)

Photojournalists **Sohrab Alam** of *Sangbad*, **Borhanuddin** from *Manav Jamin* and **Abdus Samad Jewel** from *Janakantha* were beaten by police on 2 May while photographing a demonstration by women students at Dhaka University. (Media Watch)

On the same day police in Kushtia illegally raided the house of **Tariql Haq Tariq**, local correspondent for the daily *Prothom Alo*, while he was away. Tariq is believed to have annoyed the police because his recent reports were critical of the law and order situation. (Media Watch)

On 28 May **Aminur Rahman Taj**, crime reporter with the newspaper *Ajker Kagoj*, was arrested while working in Dhaka police headquarters and charged under section 501 of the Code of Criminal Procedure for tarnishing 'the image of the police and two ladies of high rank'. Taj's arrest stems from a front-page article that denounced the wives of a minister and a high-ranking police officer for alleged corruption. **Kazi Shamed Ahmed**, Ajker Kagoj's editor, was issued with an arrest warrant after a column he wrote denounced Taj's arrest. (RSF)

BELARUS

On 28 April a KGB officer warned **Yahor Maoirchyk**, journalist for Radio Free Europe/Radio Liberty, that unless he agreed to co-operate with the intelligence services 'the same thing would happen to you as to Babitsky' (*Index* 2/2000, 3/2000). (WAN)

The authorities have refused to register the independent newspaper *Reporter*, which has been applying since early February. **Anjey Pisalnik**, a representative from *Reporter*, said the Municipal Executive Council was registering its own newspaper at the time and the independent publication was in competition. (Radio Racyja, CPJ)

Igor Irkho, a journalist with *De Facto* independent newspaper, and **Alexander Alexandrovich**, a correspondent with *Delovaya Gazeta*, were arrested on 1 May while attempting to cover an opposition rally in the town of Mogilev after they had already been assaulted by police and had a cameras damaged. (CPJ)

An attempt by weekly newspaper *Nasha Niva* to sue the State Press Committee for warning it against 'fomenting inter-ethnic enmity' was rejected on 11 May by the Supreme Economic Court. The warning followed the publication of a letter in March, entitled 'I Envy Chechnya'. The committee justified its actions claiming that 'just by looking at the title' the reader could not understand what its author, **T Sudzilouskaya**, meant. Four days later the independent was issued with a second warning for an article, entitled 'Infection of Fascism – A Lukashenka copies A Hitler'. (RFE/RL, RSF)

BRAZIL

Reporter **Claudia Bastos**, who works with TV Tapajós in Santarém, received death threats and had her home ransacked after taking an unidentified witness to the congressional investigative commission on drug trafficking in April. The witness, identified as 'Mr X', incriminated local authorities, businessmen and politicians in drugs and arms trafficking in Itaituba. Bastos is under police protection. (FIP)

BRITAIN

MI5 officers destroyed a secret tape containing potentially vital evidence of murder at the centre of 'shoot-to-kill' allegations in Northern Ireland, it was revealed on 23 May. Officers should have been prosecuted for perverting the course of justice in an attempt to cover up proof of alleged errors in an operation that resulted in the death of **Michael Tighe**, 17, and the wounding of **Martin**

McCauley, 19, after Royal Ulster Constabulary officers opened fire on them in a hayshed a few miles from Lurgan, County Armagh, in October 1982. The officers maintained they had given a warning before shooting, but McCauley rejects the claim. The shed was bugged and **John Stalker**, Manchester's deputy chief constable in charge of the investigation, thought he could use any recorded material to establish exactly what had happened. He was subsequently informed the evidence had been destroyed. It transpired later that a copy had been made of the tape which allegedly revealed no warning had been given. When the information came to light, the prospect of damning charges against MI5 activities was too much for Sir Patrick Mayhew, the then attorney-general, and Tom King, the then Northern Ireland secretary. The case was pushed under the carpet. (*Guardian*)

Teachers on 23 May warned that schools will find it more difficult to force pupils to abide by uniform codes once the Human Rights Act comes into force in October. Pupils – and their parents – will have the right to challenge bans on certain types of clothing, jewellery and even haircuts on the basis that their human rights have been infringed. (*Daily Telegraph*)

Nigel Wylde, a former army colonel, was sent for trial on 25 May under the Official Secrets Act. Wylde, 53 from Esher, Surrey, denies revealing damaging information in **Tony Geraghty**'s book, *The Irish War* (*Index* 2/1999, 2/2000). There has been

• •

NORBERT ZONGO
Conspiracy of silence

'Burkina Faso has laws against press freedom, but the Constitution has its own laws on press freedom. The government of President Blaise Compaore refused to create the *Conseil de L'Information* designated by the Constitution, but instead created their own *Conseil Superieur de L'Information*, which is not independent. In [April] 1997, the government banned all free radio discussion of social problems.

There were national elections last week [11 May 1997] for regional representatives. Not so many people voted and the pPresident banned democratic alternatives. There was so much electoral fraud! This [election-rigging] is not a surprise. There is much bribery to sway and win elections. This is well known, everybody recognises it. But the papers don't print these stories! It's not logical! These are events that journalists are obligated to report! There are about ten papers in the country, but they refuse to publish information about corruption and bribery. *L'Indépendent* is the most critical. Newspapers refuse to say what happens. There is a conspiracy of silence.

There are no official restrictions on *L'Indépendent*. Unofficially, they tried to bribe me in the first year. I worked for one paper where they did bribe the editors, so I left and created *L'Indépendent*. They came and offered me CFA50mn (US$20,000), – "just to help you," they said, with the understanding that I wouldn't be critical. One man came, I don't know his name. He said, "I agree with your writing and President Compaore does too. We want to help you." But self-censorship was implied. It was clear the man worked for the government.

I don't understand the behaviour of my peers. We don't want them to be critical necessarily, but they must say what they see, and they certainly see what is happening. I was last jailed in 1981 and 1982 for more than one year. I don't care what they do to me, because freedom is more important.' ❑

*On 13 December 1998, **Norbert Zongo**, founding editor of* L'Indépendent, *was found dead near his burned-out car some 100kms from Ouagadougo. An independent commission of inquiry found in May 1999 that he was murdered for political reasons. Six members of the presidential security regiment were named as suspects. This interview by **Keith Snow** was made in May 1997*

• •

no attempt to take an injunction out against the book. (*Daily Telegraph*)

Sinn Fein ministers **Martin McGuiness** and **Bairbre de Brun** caused controversy on 3 June by ordering the Northern Ireland departments of education and health not to fly the Union flag. (*Guardian*)

The government's Prevention of Terrorism Bill looks set to become law during the next parliamentary session. On 21 June peers refused to exempt journalists from the legislation that will require anyone with information about a terrorist act to notify the police. The amendment was rejected by a resounding majority, who appeared to agreed with the government line that journalists had a 'degree of responsibility to society'. (*Guardian*)

BURKINA FASO

President Blaise Compaoré is under attack for ignoring a government inquiry that found members of his security guard were responsible for the murder of journalist **Norbert Zongo** in November 1998 (*Index* 2/1999, 5/1999, 6/1999, 1/2000) The verdict, reported on 5 June, strengthened suspicions that Compaoré is protecting his brother from prosecution. (*West Africa*)

BURMA

On 12 May communications minister Brig Gen Win Tin told officials that it is illegal to use international telephone and email

services. 'Such illegal services could reduce the ministry's revenue,' he said. The state-run news agency is allowed to provide telephone and email services. but it cannot allow public access to the Internet. Unauthorised ownership of a modem is punishable with up to 15 years' imprisonment and a fine. (Global Internet Liberty Campaign)

It was reported on 1 June that Tourism Concern and Burma Campaign UK have called for a boycott of all Lonely Planet travel books until the guide to Burma is withdrawn. Lonely Planet has been publishing information about Burma for over 25 years. Founder Tony Wheeler said: 'The Burmese would be overjoyed if one of their most long-standing and most widely available critics were to be silenced.' (*Guardian*)

CAMBODIA

It was reported on 19 April that a group of non-profit journalists have set up a campaign called the Free Press Campaign in reaction to the use of unlawful power against journalists of print and e-news media. Their website can be found at *www.freepress.itgo.com*. (Cambodia News Bulletin)

CANADA

It was reported on 6 June that seven accredited photographers had been hit with pepper spray by Royal Canadian Mounted Police on 4 June while covering a protest against the Organisation of American States in Windsor, Ontario. **Ted Andkilde**, a freelance photographer, said: 'I

think they just didn't want us to take any more photos ... I was wearing my credentials round my neck as well as two cameras and a satchel of lenses ... He aimed the thing right in my eyes and blasted it ... It is very unlikely that he mistook me for a protestor.' (CJFE)

CHINA

Falun Gong adherents continue to fall foul of the authorities in numbers too great to record here in detail. For fully referenced information about victims of the persecution from 7 April to 7 June, please visit: www.indexoncensorship.org/news/

A villager from Shanxi province, **Li Lusong**, 20, who was arrested on 10 December last year for writing anti-corruption slogans on the walls of government buildings, had his tongue cut out after swearing at the police who were beating him. No officers have been punished. (Associated Press, Agence France-Presse, Information Centre of Human Rights and Democratic Movements in China)

An Jun from Xinyang in central China, who exposed almost 100 cases of official corruption, was sentenced to four years in prison on 20 April on charges relating to the fact that his pressure group, Corruption Watch, was not registered. (Associated Press, Agence France-Presse, Information Centre of Human Rights and Democratic Movements in China) The Chinese Central Publicity Department banned the screening in May of a 35-part TV dramatisation of the corruption scandal surrounding the disgraced Beijing Party chief, Chen Xitong (*Index* 6/1997). The drama was accused of implicating other officials, and failing to 'fully demonstrate the central leadership's determination' to tackle corruption. (*South China Morning Post*)

On 5 May the government ordered the destruction of stocks of nine books about the Zhong Gong exercise group, seven of them written by the group's founder, **Zhang Hongbao**, now in hiding (*Index* 2/2000, 3/2000). The government has also extended its ban on 'cult' groups to 14 Christian groups and the Guan Yin Method Buddhist group, all based in Taiwan. Guan Yin Method claims 500,000 members in mainland China. (Associated Press, Agence France-Presse, Reuters)

Twenty members of a religious sect in Sichuan, called 'The Disciples', were arrested on 19 May. One of the group's leaders, **Li Xueqing**, was arrested the previous week and sentenced to one year in a labour camp. His group urges followers to ignore the strict, though often flouted, single child policy. **Li Dexian**, a Christian pastor from Guangdong province who refuses to register his church with the authorities, was arrested and detained for 15 days on 11 April. He was kept in shackles and chains for much of his detention. He has been arrested 14 times since October, when his church was demolished hours before delivering his weekly sermon. **Jiang Shurang**,

a Catholic priest from Zhejiang province, was sentenced to six years in prison on 25 April for 'illegal operation' and 'illegal publishing' of Bibles. The welfare and whereabouts of five other priests arrested in the same area since January are unknown. The official press reported on 3 May that 47 members of the Protestant Quanfanwei (Full Circle) Church were arrested as part of an ongoing campaign to eradicate the group in Anhui province. Six leaders face charges under laws enacted to counter Falun Gong, eight are likely to be sent to labour camps and 22 face unspecified 'public order punishments'. It has been suggested the arrests were timed to coincide with the imminent release of the group's leader, **Xu Yongxi**, sentenced in 1997. (Associated Press, Agence France-Presse, Christian Solidarity Worldwide. Information Centre of Human Rights and Democratic Movements in China, *South China Morning Post*)

Qi Yanchen, a regular contributor to the pro-democracy, online magazine VIP Reference, was due to be sentenced following a short, closed trial in Hebei province on 23 May. Sentencing was delayed because one of the judges at the trial was unwell, but it was noted that the date coincided with a US Congressional vote on granting Permanent Normal Trading Relations. He is likely to be sentenced to around five years' imprisonment. (Associated Press, Agence France-Presse, Information Centre of Human Rights and Democratic

Movements in China, *South China Morning Post*, VIP Reference)

The government issued stern warnings to potential 'trouble-makers' in the run-up to the 11th anniversary of the Tiananmen Square Massacre of 4 June. An official circular to universities issued on 27 May warned students and staff to beware of 'black hands' undermining the leadership and spreading 'bourgeois-liberal thinking'. Several open letters by dissident groups were sent to top legal and political offices, calling for a full investigation into the events of 1989, reversal of the verdicts of 'counter-revolutionary crimes' and the release of prisoners still held. One such was issued by nine dissidents in Liaoning province on 24 May, three of whom were instantly taken into custody. **Professor Ding Zilin** (*Index* 3/2000) issued a letter signed by 108 bereaved families and had police stationed outside her residence in Beijing. In response to foreign journalists' questions, Foreign Ministry spokeswoman Zhang Qiyue ruled out the distribution of funds collected by Professor Ding and **Lois Wheeler Snow** for bereaved families, saying 'no foreign country has the right to interfere in China's internal affairs'. **Huang Qi**, founder of a website holding articles relating to the massacre, was arrested in Sichuan province on 3 June. His wife, Zeng Li, claims he is being held on charges of subversion, leading to a possible ten-year prison sentence. On the anniversary, police maintained a heavy presence arresting a lone protestor, **Shen Zhidao**, after he scattered leaflets saying 'Overthrow despotic communism' and 'Freedom, democracy, fairness, human rights'. Shen, a known supporter of the China Democratic Party, was arrested on 4 June last year having paraded the Square with an umbrella bearing similar slogans. (Associated Press, Agence France-Presse, Information Centre of Human Rights and Democratic Movements in China, *South China Morning Post*)

Feng Daxuan, a former journalist and political prisoner, was indicted on charges of subversion on 9 June for having interviewed protesting workers in Sichuan who have not been paid for a year. He could spend ten years in prison if convicted. (Associated Press, Agence France-Presse, Information Centre of Human Rights and Democratic Movements in China)

COLOMBIA

Two television crews from Caracol and RCN were shot at by unknown gunmen on 22 May while travelling down the Cimitarra river on the way back from an assignment. Despite waving their press credentials and a white flag, they were attacked twice during their journey. Nobody was hurt. (IFJ)

Reporter **Jineth Bedoya Lima** of Bogotá-based daily *El Espectador* was kidnapped, drugged and brutally beaten on 25 May by presumed members of the right-wing paramilitary group United Self-defence Forces

of Colombia (AUC). Bedoya was found lying with her hands tied on a road 113km south-east of Bogotá suffering from severe shock ten hours after the kidnapping. The journalist had gone that morning to talk to an informant in La Modelo prison on the outskirts of Bogotá about alleged death threats made by jailed AUC members against her and other journalists over coverage of a bloody riot in the prison on 27 April. Press reports had mentioned that several inmates killed during the riot may have been victims of execution-style killings by AUC prisoners. (WAN, CPJ, RSF)

Journalist **María Alejandra González Mosquera**, of Super radio in Popayán province, fled the country in early June after receiving death threats from AUC paramilitaries. (IFJ)

COTE D'IVOIRE

Five soldiers stormed through the offices of private daily *La Référence* in Abidjan on 16 May, damaging computers and arresting four staff members. The journalists, including managing editor **Patrice Pohé**, were taken to military headquarters, kicked and forced to do push-ups before being released an hour later. The incident was supposedly in reaction to two articles published on 12 and 16 May criticising the president's power base and the size of the president's wife's entourage. (WAN)

CROATIA

Three pages of transcripts of a taped conversation that took

place on 27 December 1997 between the late president Tudjman and his chief domestic affairs aide, Ivic Passalic, were published in the Easter edition of *Jutarnji list*. They show that Tudjman was determined to have control of the influential daily *Vecernji list* when it was privatised in 1997. The chief domestic affairs aide, who currently enjoys parliamentary immunity, initially tried to deny the conversations took place but finally said that if such tapes exist they were the private property of the Tudjman estate and not for public consumption. (RFE/RL)

CUBA

The 18 May issue of *Carta de Cuba* magazine reported that the State Security police raided the opening party of the independent Aurora Library in Havana in early April. The director of Aurora, **Jorge Santacana**, was arrested and detained overnight. (Friends of Cuban Libraries)

On 12 May **Felix A. Bonne Carcases** was released from custody on 'conditional liberty', to be followed on 15 May by **Marta Beatriz Roque Cabello** and **Rene Gomez Manzano** on 23 May. The three, along with economist **Vladimiro Roca Antunez**, were arrested in 1997 for writing a pro-democracy document entitled *The Homeland Belongs to All* (*Index* 8/1992, 4/1995, 2/1996, 4/1997). The four had been held for 15 months without charge or trial before eventually being charged for sedition on 15 October 1998. Roque was sentenced to three and a half years, Bonne and

Gomez to four and Roca to five. Roca, believed to have been the group's leader, is still being detained in solitary confinement. (*New York Times, Miami Herald,* UNHCR)

CZECH REPUBLIC

The 'classified' communist-era police file on foreign minister Jan Kavan has been leaked and made into a book. Interior minister Stanislav Gross said on 18 May that an investigation had been launched. (RFE/RL)

Police have brought charges against **Michal Zitko**, owner of the Otakar II publishing house which printed the first-ever unabridged Czech translation of Adolf Hitler's *Mein Kampf*. Zitko is accused of supporting a movement aimed at suppressing minorities and could face between three and eight years in prison. In a recent survey, 39% of Czechs were opposed to the sale *Mein Kampf*, 30% did not mind and 31% had no opinion. (RFE/RL)

DEMOCRATIC REPUBLIC OF CONGO

Jean-René Mputu Bidduaya, information director at the private television and radio station RAGA, and **Jean-René Lumbana Kapasa** at radio-television Kin Malebo have been forbidden from leaving Kinshasa until further notice. The authorities stated the two journalists were wanted for questioning after hosting **Antoine Gabriel Kyungu wa Kumwanza**, ambassador to Saudi Arabia, on their stations on

9 April. Kyungu, a former governor of Katanga, ssaid that people no longer had faith in the government. He was arrested a short time later in Kinshasa. On Tuesday 11 April Mputu Biduaya was briefly detained. On 14 April Mputu Biduaya and Lumbana Kapasa were interrogated by the head of state's special adviser on security matters, Nono Lutula. Mputu Biduaya was forced to hand over a cassette of the programme. (Journaliste en Danger)

Journalist **Bruno Kadima** and technician **José Mounkanda Ntumba** of the Kinshasa weekly *Umoja* were arrested and jailed on 26 April for one week for publishing two articles entitled 'Here are the first eight articles of the Accords of Lemera' and 'Slaughter at N'dijili airport – Kabila legally responsible'. In the first, which appeared on 4 April, *Umoja* published eight articles contained in the hitherto secret Accord of Lemera, signed on 23 October 1996 by the founders of the Alliance of Democratic Forces for Liberation, the group led by now President Laurent Kabila. The second article, which concerned the 14 April explosion of ammunition at Kinshasa/N'Dijili airport which killed approximately 100 people, blamed the government and said that 'a civilian airport should not serve as a munitions warehouse'. (Journaliste en Danger)

Publisher **Richard Nsamba** and editor **Matthieu Elonge Ossako** of *Le Messager Africain* disappeared on 3 May following the issuance of an arrest warrant on 27 April (*Index 3/2000*). Their

disappearance is believed to be connected with report questioning the credibility of Eastern Kasai governor Jean-Charles Okoto. (WAN)

Freddy Loseke Lisumbu La Yayenga, editor of *La Libre Afrique,* has been sentenced to three years in prison by the Court of Military Order, it was reported on 24 May (*Index 2/2000, 3/2000*). No appeal is possible but a presidential pardon would secure his release. (RSF)

Jean Kenge Mukengeshayi, editor-in-chief of the Kinshasa daily *Le Phare*, was abducted in the late afternoon on 8 June by two men in civilian clothes, who later claimed to be from Special Services. He spent the night in deplorable conditions. The same afternoon, officers had questioned the journalist over an article titled 'Country at the mercy of Mafiosi', written by **Tshivis Tshivuadi**, assistant editor and president of the NGO Journaliste en Danger. The article denounced the management of public affairs. (Journaliste en Danger)

EGYPT

On 16 April a Cairo criminal court sentenced five *Al-Ahrar* journalists to six months in prison for allegedly libelling Muhammad Fahim Al-Rayan, chairman of national carrier Egypt Air. Editor **Salah Qabadya**, cartoonist **Nabil Sadek** and reporters **Hussam Suleiman, Muhammad Abdel Fahim Alnur** and **Hisham Mostafa** were sentenced to six-month jail terms and fines of LE7,500

(US$2,100) each. The convictions stem from *Al-Ahrar's* coverage of corruption and mismanagement at Egypt Air in a long-running series of articles, entitled 'Breaches of millions within the kingdom of Egypt Air'. (WAN,CPJ)

On 28 April the Ministry of Information confiscated the latest edition of the monthly *Al Tadamon* because of its critical coverage of the embargo on Iraq. *Al Tadamon*, printed in Cyprus, was censored in 1999 over an editorial criticising the state of press freedom as a 'burlesque comedy'. (*Cairo Times*, WAN)

On 13 May state prosecutors referred **Salaheddin Mohsen**, author of *Shivering of the Lights*, to state security criminal court on charges of 'denigration of revealed religions' and 'threatening social peace' through his self-published book. The date of the hearing has been set for 17 June. (*Cairo Times*)

On 20 May the Political Parties Committee ordered the closure of the Labour Party and its newspaper, *Al-Shahab*. The committee based its decision on Article 17 which gives government power to suspend any party or newspaper perceived to be acting against the 'higher interests' of the state. The closure is seen as linked to *Al-Shahab's* concerted campaign against the publication of *Banquet for Seaweed*, by Haider Haider. The ban was widely condemned by civil rights and freedom of expression organisations. (*Cairo Times*, Egyptian Organisation of Human Rights)

On 3 June the High Constitutional Court overturned Law 153, passed in May 1999, which laid down governmental registration requirement for all NGOs operating in Egypt (*Index* 4/1999, 5/1999). The ruling comes into effect immediately and is not open to appeal. (*Cairo Times*)

FIJI

The High Court judge rejected on 26 April an application by the *Fiji Times* to quash the government's decision to deny the company's editor-in-chief, Scottish-born **Russell Hunter,** a renewed work permit (*Index* 1/2000, 2/2000). (PINA)

On 28 May, shortly after Fiji TV broadcast a discussion of George Speight's coup on the programme *Close-Up*, a mob of his supporters ransacked its premises, smashing equipment and forcing staff to flee. A panel, chaired by reporter **Riyaz Sayed-Khaiyum**, included political commentator **Jone Dakuvula** and Communications Fiji Ltd managing director **William Parkinson**, who were both critical of the rebels. (Fiji TV, University of the South Pacific)

FRANCE

Images of untried defendants in handcuffs and victims of crime will be banned from the press and television under a law passed by the Senate on 30 May. The media are already constrained by some of the world's harshest privacy laws and this latest ruling provoked cries of 'censorship' from journalists. The law also bans media from showing pictures of victims of violence if the image is likely to 'jeopardise the dignity of the person portrayed'. Infringement of the law will carry a maximum £9,500 (US$14,060) fine. (*Guardian*)

GEORGIA

Akaki Gogichaishvili, who anchors the popular weekly programme *60 Minutes* on independent channel Rustavi 2, told a 19 May press conference that he had repeatedly been threatened by officials and businessmen (including members of President Eduard Shevardnadze's family), who were angered by the show's hard-hitting investigations of corruption and the criminal underworld. Gogichaishvili claimed he had received death threats. The harassment peaked after the 26 March and 2 April broadcasts of two episodes alleging corruption in the Georgian Writers' Union. (RSF)

GUATEMALA

A photographer for Guatemala City daily *Prensa Libre* was killed and two other journalists were wounded when private security guards opened fire on rioters on on 27 April. The dead man, **Roberto Martinez**, was shot twice. **Christian Alejandro Garcia**, cameraman for Channel 7's *Notisiete*, and **Julio Cruz**, a reporter for the daily *Siglo Ventiuno*, were both injured. Local sources reported a total of 16 casualties. The two security guards responsible were detained by journalists and handed over to the police. (CPJ, WAN)

FIJI TV
Audience participation

Fiji TV: *Do you think George Speight has been given too much prominence?*
Parkinson: I think the local media was in the middle of the drama and, yes, George Speight got a lot of coverage. But as time has gone on, the local media has started to see the issues.

Do you think access should have been denied to media?
Davukula: Overseas, they would have closed off the parliamentary complex. Here, it's different and I think that's probably a legacy of 1987, which was also a fairly 'open' coup.

But we also saw in 1987 that once the media started making reports that were critical of the coup-makers, they were shut down.
Parkinson: You have to acknowledge ... the support for Speight and his followers, at least from certain areas of the country; you can't deny that. Media ethics would normally say, 'No, we will not provide a platform for someone who has committed a crime.' But if we were to deny him that platform, it could lead to further violence from his supporters.
Davukula: Those who campaigned against the Chaudhry government in the last year have convinced the grassroots that there's a huge threat to Fijians, that we must get rid of this government, or lose everything. That's the sympathy Fijians have for this coup, but it's going to wear off once the naked interest is revealed.

What is the 'naked interest'?
Davukula: The naked interest is a bunch of people who want to get to power through unlawful means: they couldn't get it through the constitution so they want it through a coup, and they want to impose a system of government in the name of indigenous rights. But it does not accord with the Fijian way of thinking, which is a peaceful and consensual way, give and take, listening and respectful ... This is very un-Fijian. ❏

*On 28 May, after the transmission of a discussion of the coverage of George Speight's coup, a mob of his supporters ransacked Fiji TV, smashing equipment and forcing staff to flee. This is an edited transcript of part of the programme chaired by reporter **Riyaz Sayed-Khaiyum**. Panellists included political commentator **Jone Dakuvula** and Communications Fiji Ltd managing director **William Parkinson***

The government suspended the Telecommunications Law on 5 May in direct response to a damning report by the Organisation of American States on 14 April which exposed a de facto monopoly in television ownership and government involvement in the closure of a number of critical print and broadcast outlets. (Guatemalan Journalists Association, AMARC)

Four reporters for the Guatemala City daily *El Periodico* were threatened or intimidated while the newspaper was preparing to publish an investigative article about secret intelligence operations that saw the light on 15 May. The article described an intelligence agency run by the Presidential High Command under the direction of retired military officer, Jacobo Salán Sánchez. (Centro para la Defensa de Libertad de Expressión)

HONDURAS

On 26 April two unidentified men shot **Julio César Pineda**, co-ordinator of the press department of Radio Progresso in El Progresso near San Pedro Sula. Pineda survived but was left crippled and bleeding. He had received threatening phone calls prior to the murder attempt and his wife claims she is still being followed by unidentified individuals. In the months leading up to the attack, Radio Progresso had documented cases of malpractice in El Progresso's hospital, denounced the Honduras Medical Association for refusing to work with a Cuban medical brigade after

Hurricane Mitch, and opposed a bus fare increase. Pineda also represented Radio Progresso on a joint commission investigating executions of gang members. (CPJ)

INDIA

N. Biren Singh, editor of the vernacular-language daily *Naharlogi Thoudang*, and 84-year-old activist **Thounaojam Iboyaima** were arrested on 14 April by police in Imphal, Manipur, because an allegedly seditious speech by Iboyaima had been published in Singh's paper. Singh and Iboyaima were charged on 15 April with sedition and related offences. (RSF, CPJ)

On 15 April a landmine exploded near Radio Kashmir, the local branch of All India Radio, in Srinagar. Officials believe that the station was targeted because of its criticism of separatist groups. (RSF)

On 17 May the lower house of parliament adopted the Information Technology Bill after a brief three-hour debate. The bill allows policemen to make searches without a warrant and close down any cybercafé if they think a 'crime' might be committed there. Anyone who runs an 'anti-Indian' website – a vague notion that includes pornographic and 'subversive' websites – faces a maximum sentence of five years in jail. The following day the government presented a draft bill that could replace the Terrorist and Disruptive Activities Act. According to the current proposals, journalists would be

obliged to pass to the police any information concerning 'terrorist activities', or face a maximum of three years in jail. (RSF)

Recent Publications: *Persecuted for challenging injustice: Human Rights Defenders in India* (AI, April 2000, pp 96); *Punitive use of preventive detention legislation in Jammu and Kashmir* (AI, May 2000, pp 34).

INDONESIA

A journalist from MS Tri FM radio station, **Evangel Kawatub**, was badly beaten by police at an anti-Suharto demonstration on 30 March on Jalan Teuku Umar in central Jakarta. (Pacific Media Watch)

On 2 April a journalist and senior editor with *Menara* tabloid **Hoesin Kalahapan** (*Index* 3/2000) was kidnapped while researching an article on the misuse of the government's reafforestation fund. He was hung upside down, beaten in the face and stomach for eight days and then abandoned in Pulomas, East Jakarta. This was the third attack on Kalahapan since his first article on the subject appeared in *Menara*. On 21 February he was held and beaten and on 9 March he was threatened with death. The Commission for Missing Persons suspects that the abduction was ordered by the governor of West Kalimantan. (Pacific Media Watch)

On 6 May about 30 members of Banser, the paramilitary youth wing of the 30-million-strong Nahdlatul Ulama (NU) forced their way into the offices of the daily *Jawa Pos* threatening staff and disrupting the Sunday edition. They were reacting to an article that alleged that President Wahid's government and leading NU members practised 'corruption, collusion and nepotism'. Despite an apology by managing editor **Dahlan Iskan**, Wahid accused the paper on 8 May of 'conspiracy to topple and discredit the government'. (CPJ)

IRAN

It was reported that on 17 April the outgoing parliament had approved a set of provisions that would give conservative elements new controls over the media. Several articles require all newspaper licences to be approved by the Intelligence Ministry, the courts and the police – all conservative strongholds – instead of the more reform-minded Culture Ministry. (WAN)

Six participants at a Berlin conference, held to debate the aftermath of February's parliamentary elections, were arrested on their return to Iran. Lawyer **Mehranguis Kaar**, publisher **Shahla Lahiji**, journalist **Akbar Ganji**, student leader **Ali Afshari**, a former minister and director of *Iran Tomorrow*, **Ezzatollah Sahabi** (*Index* 1/1999) and editor **Hamed-Reza Jalai Pour** (*Index* 5/1998) were detained on 29 April by the Islamic Revolutionary Court. Another participant, **Ayatollah Hassan Youssefi Eshkevari**, was arrested on 25 April. Two others, MP-elect **Jamileh Kadivare** and *Sobh-e Emrooz* editorial member **Ali-Reza-Tabar**, were charged with 'distributing propaganda

against the Islamic Republic' at the conference. They were later released on bail. (PEN, HRW)

Between 20 April and 9 May, 17 newspapers, weeklies and other publications were closed by the judiciary. *Jebneh* weekly, *Mosharekat* daily, *Sobh-e Emrooz* daily, *Payam-e* daily, *Azad* daily, *Arya* daily, *Aftab-e Emrooz* daily, *Akhbar-e Eghtesad* daily, *Asr-e Azadegan* daily, *Fatth* daily, *Payam-e Hajar*, *Aban*, *Iran-e farda*, *Ava*, *Arzesh*, *Bamdad-e No* daily and *Gozaresh-e Rouz* daily were closed and their editors were arrested for publishing material that had 'disparaged Islam and the religious elements of the Islamic revolution'. (WAN, *Guardian*)

On 2 April **Akbar Ganji** (*Index* 3/1998) was imprisoned by the Press Court for a series of articles in which he alleged that top intelligence officials were behind the serial murders of secular intellectuals (*Index* 1/1999, 2/1999, 3/1999). He has been sent to solitary confinement at the notorious Evin prison. On 27 April eight of the 22 people accused of the recent serial killings of intellectuals were freed on 'clear proof' that they were not guilty. (*International Herald Tribune*, ADHRI)

On 1 May journalist **Emadeddin Baghi** of *Fatth* daily went on trial accused of criticising the application of the death penalty, 'endangering national security' and 'writing falsehoods'. (ADHRI)

On 16 May the Tehran Press Court was reported to have ordered the closure of the

newspaper *Ham'mihan*, run by the former mayor of Iran, **Gholamhossein Karbaschi** (*Index* 3/1998, 5/1998). (WAN)

Courtroom proceedings in the trial for espionage of 13 Iranian Jews and eight Iranian Muslims ended on 13 June (*Index* 3/2000). Hossein Ali Amiri, the judiciary chief of Fars province, said the court was awaiting responses to two unspecified inquiries and would then issue a verdict within a week. Eight of the 13 Jewish defendants have pleaded guilty, four pleaded innocent and one has said he passed information to Israel, but did not think his action constituted espionage. Israel denied that any of the 13 was a spy. Attention has focused on the fairness of a closed trial with no jury and the judge acting as prosecutor. (Associated Press)

IRAQ

On 1 June **Sarbast Mahmood**, editor of *Medya* newspaper, was found murdered on the outskirts of Irbil, capital of southern Kurdistan. No one claimed responsibility. The incident occured at a time when the two main Kurdish parties, the KDP and the PUK, were engaged in a media war. (*Kurdish Media*)

KAZAKHSTAN

The 27 April issue of the opposition weekly *XXI Vek* was confiscated without explanation by Almaty tax police, according to editor **Bigeldy Gabdullin**. The paper has repeatedly been subjected to official pressure (*Index* 1/2000, 2/2000). (RFE/RL)

Ramazan Esergepov, editor of the Almaty-based weekly *Nachnem s Ponedelnkia*, told journalists on 16 May that municipal officials are trying to evict the newspaper. On 25 May, over 30 policemen stormed the editorial office and confiscated all 53,000 copies of the weekly's print run, together with other documents. Esergepov said the pressure is in response to recent articles criticising Almaty mayor Viktor Khrapunov. Printers report they have been ordered not to publish *Nachnem s Ponedelnika*, along with the newspapers *Do i Posle Ponedelnika* and *Ponedelnik*, which Esergepov launched after the 25 May raid. Since 11 October 1998, *Nachnem s Ponedelnika* has been sued 17 times for defamation. (RFE/RL, CPJ)

On 24 May film-maker **Rashid Nugmanov**, a member of the opposition Republican People's Party, was detained at Almaty airport on his arrival from France, where he has lived for the past seven years, and ordered to report to the tax police the following day. (RFE/RL)

KENYA

Two policemen assaulted journalist **Victor Nzuma** of the *Daily Nation* on 9 May, destroying his camera and threatening to shoot him. He was taking pictures of the policemen arresting shareholders of the Mavoloni Company Ltd. (NDIMA)

Reporters **Amos Majisu** and **Vincent Maluti** from the daily *People* were arrested on 12 June and questioned over an article which alleged that police officers in Kakamega had raped three women in Malava on 24 May. According to later reports, no rape had actually occurred: the women had bribed their potential attackers, and later contacted the journalists to denounce them. Majisu and Maluti were asked to report to the Criminal Investigation Division in Kakamega where they were subjected to a day's interrogation. They were later released without charge pending further investigation. (CPJ)

A group of students from Jomo Kenyatta University attacked the offices of the *Daily Nation* in Nairobi on 12 June, following an article in that day's paper which said that drugs were 'freely available' on campus. They broke windows and computers in the attack. (RSF)

KYRGYZSTAN

Viktor Zapolsky, editor-in-chief of the independent weekly *Delo*, said in mid-May that he plans to sue the State Tax Inspectorate in a bid to overturn a demand for 1.3 million som (about US$27,000) in back taxes. The weekly published several articles in favour of opposition politician **Felix Kulov** during and after the last presidential elections (*Index* 3/2000). (RFE/RL)

Guild of Prisoners of Conscience Chairman Topchubek Turgunaliev said on 25 May that the Ministry of Justice had refused to register the organisation on the grounds no one is persecuted for political motives in Kyrgyzstan.

RFE/RL)

The Washington-based International Women's Media Foundation gave its annual award for 2000 to journalist **Zamira Sydykova**, who founded the independent weekly *Res Publica* in February 1992. She was given an 18-month suspended sentence in July 1995 for allegedly libelling President Askar Akayev. In 1997, she was again sentenced to 18 months' imprisonment, for allegedly libelling a manager at the state gold company. She was released in August 1997 after two months in jail. After continued official harassment (*Index* 3/1999, 4/1999, 5/1999, 2/2000, 3/2000), *Res Publica* ceased publishing on 28 March 2000. On 8 June Bishkek City Court overturned a 31 March ruling fining *Res Publica* 50,000 som (US$1,000) for insulting the former chairman of the Kyrgyz Committee for Human Rights. (RFE/RL)

LEBANON

It was reported on 7 June that the BBC has demanded that Israel pay compensation to the family of driver **Abed Takkoush**, who was killed on 23 May by an Israeli tank incendiary round while working with reporter **Jeremy Bowen** near Bint Jbeil, southern Lebanon. The BBC and Amnesty International said there was no fighting in the area at the time. Senior members of the Israeli Defence Force said that 'things don't look that good' for the army after the BBC sent a live videotape of Takkoush's death. (*Times*)

Simon Davies on

PRIVACY

Ursula Owen on

HATE SPEECH

Patricia Williams on

RACE

Gabriel Garcia Marquez on

JOURNALISM

John Naughton on

THE INTERNET

...all in **INDEX**

LUXEMBOURG

Journalists expressed concern on 2 June after undercover police posed as reporters to lure a gunman out of a nursery school where he had been holding 20 children and their teachers hostage. The man was shot dead with a gun reportedly concealed in a fake camera. (IFJ)

MEXICO

On 28 April **José Ramírez Puente**, director of the Ciudad Juárez-based news programme *Juárez Hoy* broadcast on Radio Net, was found next to his car with 30 knife wounds in his body and eight kg of marijuana in the boot. Neither the journalist nor his station had received any recent threats. In March, Ramírez Puente had investigated a story on prostitution in Ciudad Juárez. On 9 April **Pablo Pineda**, reporter and photographer for *La Opinión*, was also found dead. He had reported on the cross-border drug trade (*Index 3/2000*). (RSF)

Concern is mounting about the federal prosecution of **Melitón García**, a reporter for Monterey-based daily *El Norte*, who is being charged for fraudulently obtaining a voter credential. If convicted he faces up to six years in jail. The charges stem from a two-part series, published in *El Norte* on 16 and 17 May, in which the journalist reported on his own efforts to obtain a voting credential using a false birth certificate. García described how 'coyotes', or unofficial 'document expediters', who congregate outside government offices, sell false birth certificates for 1,100

pesos (US$100). In referring the case to the special prosecutor, the Federal Electoral Institute argued that García is being prosecuted for his illegal actions, not for his journalism. (CPJ)

MOROCCO

On 14 April the authorities dismissed directors **Larbi Belarbi**, **Mustafa Mellouk** and **Mohammad Mamadof** from public TV station 2M after its weekly press programme reported on an edition of the French weekly *Le Journal*, which ran an interview with Polisario Front leader Mohammed Abdel Aziz. On 15 April the government banned national distribution of *Le Journal* and its Arabic stablemate *Al-Sahifa* – both printed in France – although *Al-Sahifa* did not carry the controversial interview. An official statement ascribed the ban to 'excesses in editorial line…'. *Le Journal* has distinguished itself by taking outspoken positions on taboo issues of the day. (*Middle East International*, CPJ, RSF)

On 26 April a court sentenced **Mustafa Alaoui**, editor of the Arabic-language weekly *Al-Ousaba*, to three months in prison for libelling foreign minister Muhammad Ben Aissa. His conviction arises from an investigative report of Ben Aissa's alleged involvement in embezzling money while ambassador to the US. Alaoui was also suspended from journalism for three years and fined a crippling US$100,000 in damages. (*Middle East International*)

On 27 April **Khaled Meshbal**, editor of the weekly *Al-Shamal*, was convicted of libelling foreign minister Muhammad Ben Aissa in an article in February in which he was depicted as having profited from his office. Khaled was given a three-month suspended sentence, banned from journalism for one year and ordered to pay US$12,000 in damages. (*Middle East International*, CPJ)

MOZAMBIQUE

Metical editor **Carlos Cardoso** was interrogated by officials of the attorney-general's office on 2 June and asked to reveal the source of a leaked letter published on 25 and 26 May. The letter, apparently written by assistant attorney-general Afonso Antunes, was sent to *Metical* by an anonymous source. It referred to banking fraud and the authorities' failure to prosecute suspects in the case. (MISA)

NIGERIA

Soni Daniel and **Tony Ita Etim**, reporters with *Punch* magazine, were assaulted by security aides attached to Akwa Ibom state governor Victor Attah in the week of 29 May. The reporters had been at the governor's office to cover a story. (Independent Journalism Centre)

The Nigerian Union of Journalists is to raise the entry requirements for students reading journalism, it was reported on 29 May. Students will now be required to complete a Higher National Diploma or first degree in journalism instead of an Ordinary National Diploma.

NUJ chairman Alhaji Salodoye Adewole said the change is designed to stop 'half-baked practitioners who had been dragging the image of the profession in the mud'. (Independent Journalism Centre)

PAKISTAN

Poet **Aftab Hussain** fled to New Delhi in early April after intelligence officials demanded to know why he had published *Hum Jang na Hone Denge* (We will Not let War Happen), a collection of poems written by Prime Minister **Atal Bihari Vajpayee** and released during the latter's historic state visit to Lahore in February 1999. Hussain alleges that he was ordered to make a false statement that the book had been published on the orders of deposed prime minister Nawaz Sharif. (*Daily Telegraph*)

Armed attackers severely damaged the offices of the daily *Shaam* in Hyderabad on 26 April, allegedly after an article by editor **Naz Sehto** which highlighted scandals relating to the leaders of certain political parties. (Pakistan Press Foundation)

On 2 May **Sufi Mohamed Khan**, an investigative reporter with the Urdu-language daily *Ummat Karachi*, was murdered by a gunman and two accomplices. According to Khan's editor, the attack came as a result of a mid-April article in which Khan alleged that a man named Ayaz Khatak was involved in drug trafficking. Khatak subsequently warned Khan to stop writing about his activities. Khan filed a further story about Khatak's alleged involvement with a prostitute which ran on the day he was killed. Ayaz Khatak and two other suspects are currently in police custody. (CPJ)

Despite calling for a change in the procedure for registering blasphemy charge, which would have made it harder to file a complaint, General Pervez Musharraf backed down on 17 May after Islamic groups threatened to hold protest rallies and organise strikes. Under the change, anyone with a blasphemy grievance would have had to register a complaint or First Information Report with the district commissioner, instead of with their local police chief. (*Fides, Daily Telegraph*)

On 18 May a violent mob, protesting against the murder of leading Islamic scholar **Maulana Yousef Ludhianvi** that morning, ransacked and set on fire the offices of the Karachi business daily *Business Recorder*. Although no reason was given for the attack, **Arshad Zuberi**, the paper's chief executive, claims that it looked well organised and deliberate. (Pakistan Press Foundation)

Iqbal Hussain, Kurram district correspondent for the daily *Jang* and News International, was issued with an arrest warrant on 23 May. Hussain went underground and his brother **Ajmal Hussain**, a journalist with the daily *Sahafat*, was arrested along with their father. Though both have since been released, the police have said that they will rearrest them if Hussain does not give himself up.

Hussain's troubles apparently stem from reports he had written on the arrest of a group of people during a demonstration in favour of a religious scholar in conflict with the authorities. (RSF)

Mohamed Enam Wak, an Afghan writer and prominent member of the nationalist party Afghan Mellat living in Peshawar, was shot and wounded by a hooded gunman on 1 June. The shooting appears to have been triggered by the publication of his book *Afghanistan: Federation System*, in which he debated the formation of a federal state on the basis of ethnic identity. (AI)

Ahmed Jan Siddiqui, correspondent of the newspaper *Ausaf* in Sadda, was arrested on 7 June for publishing articles denouncing corruption within the local administration. (RSF)

PALESTINE

On 17 April **Abdallah Issa**, freelance correspondent of the London-based daily *al-Sharq al-Awsat*, was arrested by the General Intelligence Service (GIS). General Amin al-Hindy claimed on 5 May that Issa was in fact a GIS officer who had 'contacted some newspapers abroad and gave out information that offended some Palestinian personalities, and harmed the relationship with friendly states'. Issa had written a number of articles unfavourable to the PA in recent months, including an interview with Palestine Minister of Solidarity Intesar al Wazir in which al Wazir questioned Arafat's authority. Issa began a hunger strike on 10 May.

(Palestine Human Rights Monitoring Group, RSF)

It was announced on 5 May that **Omar Assaf**, an organiser of public school teachers who recently ended a strike, was arrested without warrant at his house in Ramallah. Assaf's wife said she was told by police that the arrest was due to remarks on a local radio station regarding the teachers' demands. On 4 May police had closed the station Voice of Peace and Love because of the interview with Assaf. It was allowed to resume broadcasting five days later. (Palestine Human Rights Monitoring Group, CPJ, LAW]

Six journalists were injured on 15 May while covering clashes between protesters and Israeli troops. **Maher Abu Khater** and **Rabhi Al Koubari** of Wattan TV and **Jadi Ali** of Peace and Love were shot during the clashes in the West Bank while, in Gaza, **Najib Abu Al Jabin**, **Talal Abu Rahman** and **Ahmad Jadallah** also received gunshot wounds. (IFJ)

On 21 May Security Forces closed down Wattan TV two minutes before the evening news broadcast. The station was not given a reason, nor was it allowed to display a caption to explain what had happened. It is believed the closure was to prevent the broadcast of the funeral of killed PFLP activist **Issa Abed**, in which anti-authority sentiments had been voiced. On 23 May Minister of Information Yasser Abed Rabbo told Wattan TV it could resume broadcasting but, after only a few minutes, police

appeared, ordered it closed again and arrested manager **Omar Nazzal**, saying they did not recognise the ministry's authority. This was the fifth time the station had been closed since it opened in 1996. (IFJ, CPJ)

It was reported on 30 May that police officers from the Criminal Investigation Unit ordered the closure of Ramallah-based Al-Nasser TV and its sister radio station, Al-Menara. No reasons were given, but it may have been in response to a talk-show during which Palestinian Legislative Council (PLC) members had criticised the government. The following day Al-Menara was allowed to reopen. (WAN)

In late May police arrested **Fathi Barqawi**, director of news programming for the Voice of Palestine radio station. Police had reportedly accused Barqawi of 'incitement' and 'defaming the president.' (WAN)

On 1 June police ordered the closure of Bethlehem-based Al-Mahid TV without explanation, and arrested its owner **Samir Qomssiyah**. The closure and arrest may be due to a letter sent by Qomssiyah, as head of the unofficial Union of Private Radio and Television Broadcasters in Palestine, in which he protested against PA's recent clampdown on TV and radio stations in the West Bank. (CPJ)

It was reported on 1 June that PLC delegate **Hassan Khureische** was arrested, apparently for 'insulting' Arafat on a TV show. (IPI)

Freelance journalist **Maher Alami** was arrested on 6 June by the GIS because of his critical articles in the Gaza-based newspaper *Al-Istiqlaal*. (Palestine Human Rights Monitoring Group)

PANAMA

On 25 May Attorney-General José Antonio Sossa ordered that **Carlos Singares**, editor of the *El Siglo* daily, be detained for eight days for publishing a report 'whose content is an attack on [the attorney-general's] dignity, honour and decency'. On 24 May *El Siglo* had accused Sossa of applying pressure on Prosecutor Roberto Murgas Torraza, and 'forcing him to make a ruling that went against his principles' in a defamation case. Torraza later resigned, denouncing the 'institutional terrorism' and pressure he had been subjected to by Sossa. (RSF)

PARAGUAY

Two radio stations were closed down and four journalists arrested following the state of emergency declared by the government in response to the attempted coup on 18 and 19 May. The offices of Radio Asunción were ransacked and shut down by security forces on 19 May, and owners **Miguel Fernández** and **Adriana Fernández** detained as suspected sympathisers of former General Lino Oviedo, one of the alleged authors of the failed *putsch*. On the same day, Radio Yvytyruzú in Villarica region was also closed and its director, **Gustavo Musi**, forced to go into hiding. Police also arrested **Juan Carlos**

Bernabé, owner and director of Radio Nanawa and a known Oviedo supporter. On 20 May, daily *Ultima Hora* correspondent **Albert Robles** was allegedly detained and questioned for several hours. Finally, President Luis Angel González Macchi ordered the arrest of daily *ABC Color* reporter **Hugo Ruiz Olazar** for allegedly participating in the coup. Ruiz, who is also a correspondent with Agence France-Presse and Argentine daily *Clarín*, went into hiding in *ABC Color*'s offices. (RSF)

PERU

Bank accounts and four properties belonging to publishing house Editora Correo were seized under orders of a Lima court 24 hours before the general election on 9 April. The action followed a libel suit filed by ruling party congressman Miguel Ciccia Vásquez against daily *Correo de Piura*, published by Editora Correo in south Peru. Vásquez, a former member of the opposition Unión por el Perú who was accused two years ago of selling out to the government, has another libel case pending against the daily for nearly US$600,000 in damages. *Correo de Piura* editor **Rolando Rodrich Sarango** said that the paper has five such cases pending against it. (IPYS)

Journalist **Hernán Carrión de la Cruz**, who heads the *Ancash en la Noticia* news programme on Radio Ancash in the port of Chimbote, narrowly escaped being shot by an unidentified gunman on 3 April. He subsequently received threatening calls and his programme was

suspended on 25 May in what is seen as an attempt by authorities to silence the journalist's critical coverage of President Alberto Fujimori's government. After the programme broadcast a vox pop unfavourable to Fujimori in the lead-up to April's presidential election, the regional tax office allegedly harassed Radio Ancash's owner **Dante Moreno** over tax records, threatening him with a heavy fine. Moreno took the hint and asked Carrión to 'take some rest', pulling the programme off the air. (CPJ, IPYS)

On election day, 9 April, a crew from Panamericana Televisión station covering a rally supporting opposition candidate Alejandro Toledo was attacked by a group of unidentified assailants inside a TV van. Two assistant cameramen sustained cuts and bruises. (IPYS)

Journalist **Perla Diana Villanueva Pérez**, a Trujillo-based correspondent of independent television station Canal N, reported that she and her sister had been persistently harassed by unknown individuals for two weeks, starting 7 April. The two women were followed by armed men and threatened in the street, and Villanueva was photographed. Canal N is considered by many as the only channel that provided truly independent coverage of the April elections. (IPYS)

The Institute for Press and Society reported on 22 May that the email messages it regularly sends out to report press freedom abuses had been systematically blocked since March. The press rights group claims it received no

mail administrator warnings of messages not being delivered. (IPYS)

A live broadcast by independent TV station Canal N of an ill-received speech by President Fujimori in the city of Arequipa on 22 May was interrupted after unidentified individuals cut the station's satellite transmission cable. The cable was severed into five pieces half an hour into the speech, when loud protests from a vocal group of anti-Fujimori demonstrators began to dominate proceedings. Canal N correspondent **Carlos Torres Salas** was later assaulted by supporters of Fujimori's Peru 2000 electoral campaign. (IPYS)

Despite being dismissed by the public prosecutor in charge, fraud charges against independent daily *El Comercio* have yet to be filed away following the intervention of the Ministry of Industry. The charges refer to the alleged misuse of preferential exchange rate dollars more than ten years ago, and are based on accusations made by *El Comercio*'s disgruntled former general manager, Luis García Miró Elguera – allegedly as part of a plot by pro-government shareholders to take control of the paper (*Index* 3/2000). Jorge Sanz Quiros, the ad hoc prosecutor investigating dollar scam involving Peru's exchange rate market, ruled on 20 March that the case against *El Comercio* lacked sufficient evidence and violated the statute of limitations. However, two appeals since lodged by the Ministry of Industry have stopped the case from being scrapped. (IPYS)

Journalist **Fabián Salazar Olivares** was tortured on 24 May by four alleged members of the National Intelligence Service (SIN), shortly after receiving politically sensitive evidence implicating high-ranking government officials and members of the tabloid press with SIN chief Vladimiro Montesinos – a close adviser to President Fujimori. Salazar, who writes for independent daily *La República*, received five videos, three computer disks and documents from a source close to SIN. However, it seems that secret agents were tipped off when Salazar made a call on his mobile phone to arrange to take the material to the election observer team of the Organisation of American States. Ten minutes later, four men tricked their way into his office, bound him to a chair, beat him and cut his wrist down to the bone with a saw to extract information from him. The assailants then took off with the material. On 31 May, Salazar left Peru after being discharged from hospital, fearing reprisals for having spoken out about the attack. (IPYS, CPJ, RSF, IFJ)

Luis Delgado Aparicio, second vice-president in the National Congress, threatened independent radio programme *Ondas de Libertad* with legal action for having appealed for a boycott of the discredited run-off elections of 28 May. Delgado said that the attorney-general's office would 'take care' of Radio 1160, which broadcasts the current affairs programme, for having dared to interfere with the electoral process – a violation, he added, that carries a prison

sentence of between three to ten years. *Ondas de Libertad* is headed by journalist **César Hildebrant**, an outspoken critic of corruption in President Fujimori's government (*Index* 2/1998, 4/1998, 4/1999, 6/1999, 2/2000, 3/2000). (IPYS)

Several journalists at Lima-based Radio Santa Rosa have been harassed over the past few months for the station's critical stance towards the government. On 29 May **Leddy Mozombite Linares**, who hosts the women's radio programme *Sonco Warmi*, was attacked on leaving work by four men who tried to tear her clothes off. Another tried to grab her later as he indecently exposed himself. On 24 May Radio Santa Rosa reporter **Jaime Pedroza Ruiz** was grabbed and beaten in the street by two men. (IPYS)

Officers of special operations police stopped two journalists on 30 May from filming a large deployment of troops and police in a district of Chimbote city, Ancash province. Freelancer **Hugo Meza** and daily *Liberación* correspondent **Marilú Gambini** narrowly escaped being arrested and having their filming equipment confiscated. According to Gambini, the section they were shooting in had been cordoned off by authorities since the day before the 28 May election to contain student demonstrations against alleged electoral fraud. (IPYS)

Journalist and opposition congressman **Antonio Llerena Marotti** was sacked on 31 May from El Sol radio station where he had been broadcasting the

independent news programme *El Sol en la Noticia* for more than 28 years. Management cited business reasons for the dismissal, but Llerena claims it was a political move. (IFJ)

PHILIPPINES

On 14 May the publisher of the *Pagadian City Star*, William 'Billy' Yap Yu, was shot dead by an assassin in Pagadian City, Mindanao. Witnesses saw the gunman talking casually to unidentified army men on their way to the army's First Infantry Division in Pulacan, Labangan. According to a police report on 7 June the murder was related to a real estate deal. (RSF)

POLAND

The Warsaw District Court ruled on 22 May that the right-wing daily *Zycie* slandered President Aleksander Kwasnieski when it published a report in 1997 alleging that he had met with a Russian spy one year before taking office. President Kwasnieski wanted the court to fine *Zycie* 2.5m zlotys (US$555,000) in damages but it refrained from doing so. The newspaper submitted to the court hotel bills showing that the president and his family were staying in the same hotel as the spy at the same time but Kwasnieski's lawyers presented an Irish visa stamp in his passport and a letter from British Airways confirming that he had taken a flight to Ireland at the time of the alleged meeting. (RFE/RL)

RUSSIA

On 11 May, four days after Vladimir Putin's inauguration as president, armed men raided the head office of the Media-MOST organisation which owns NTV, Ekho Moskvy radio, the daily *Segodnya* and weekly news magazine *Itogi*. The authorities claimed the operation was carried out after an investigation into financial irregularities by owner **Vladimir Gusinsky**, who supported the opposition in the March presidential election and whose programmes regularly criticised Russia's performance in the Chechen war. It was reported on 14 June that Gusinsky was asked to go to the prosecutor general's office to answer questions about possessing ammunition for a gun he had been given. Two hours later an investigator emerged to inform Gusinsky's companion that he was being held overnight on fraud charges. A spokesman for the prosecutor's office said: 'Gusinsky, along with some leaders of the federal government firm Ruskote Video, extracted property worth no less than £6.8m (US$10.06m) from government ownership.' (IFJ, RFE/RL, *Daily Telegraph*)

Journalist **Alexander Yefremov** of the Siberian newspaper *Nashe Vremya* became the 14th journalist to be killed in Chechnya since September 1999 when the jeep he was travelling in towards Grozny was attacked on 12 May near the village of Kirov, killing him and two Russian police officers. (WAN, RSF)

An unknown person with a hammer attacked **Igor Domnekov**, a journalist with the twice-weekly independent newspaper *Novaia Gazeta*, outside his apartment on 12 May. The newspaper is no stranger to harassment. On 15 March, during the presidential campaign, an entire issue was destroyed by a computer hacker and a regional editor-in-chief was arrested in Perm for 'abuse of authority' before being released shortly afterwards. The magazine received warnings from the Ministry of Information for publishing an interview with Chechen President Aslan Maskhadov on 27 April. (WAN, CPJ)

Independent Chechen journalist **Tassia Issayeva** was arrested in North Ossetia near the Georgia border on 1 June during a police inspection in the village of Zaramaga. Issayeva, who apparently freelanced for international press agencies, stands accused of reporting for the official Chechen press agency. Her video camera and computer were seized. (RSF)

RWANDA

The Belgian-born Italian journalist **George Ruggiu**, who worked for Radio-Télévision Libre des Mille Collines in 1994, was jailed for 12 years on 16 May after pleading guilty before the UN International Criminal Tribunal for Rwanda to inciting genocide. Ruggiu faced two counts of directly and publicly inciting genocide. Though he did not specifically call for people to be killed, he had accused the

Belgian army of plotting with Tutsi rebels. (*Financial Times*)

SAUDI ARABIA

It was reported on 17 April that the authorities in Mecca have shut down a women-only Internet café after a complaint was filed that the cafe had been used for 'immoral purposes'. (BBC)

SERBIA-MONTENEGRO

The use of mobile phones was banned in government offices on 11 May as part of a move to protect official secrets against 'foreign spies and their local agents'. (RFE/RL)

Studio B TV, the mass-circulation daily *Blic* and RadioB2-92 were raided by police in the early hours of 17 May. **Dragan Kojadinovic**, former director of the opposition television station run by the Serbia Renewal Movement, said that the incident was a 'state-organised robbery, without any legal basis'. Witnesses said busloads of police entered the building, broke into the offices and refused entry to *Blic* staff. On the previous day the Borba publishing house, which is close to the regime, refused to print *Blic*. (RFE/RL, ANEM)

A military court in Nis ordered the rearrest of **Miroslav Filipovic** on 22 May for 'espionage' and 'spreading false information' as a result of several articles he wrote for the independent daily *Danas*. A military prosecutor asked the court to order Filipovic's return to the detention from which he

GEORGES RUGGIU
The horrible truth

Georges Ruggiu: Madam President, when I had the opportunity to participate in many interviews with the Office of the Prosecutor, I realised that some persons in Rwanda had been killed during the events of 1994, and that there was a direct link with what I had said, and their deaths. Under these circumstances, I believed that I had no other honest choice than to plead guilty. Please be aware that these are events which I regret, but which did indeed occur, and I have decided to assume responsibility.

Q: *Your counsel spoke of threats and pressure exerted upon you by other detainees in the UN Detention Facility (UNDF). How did these threats and pressure influence your decision to change your plea?*

Ruggiu: These threats simply enabled me to react. I realised that the reason was to stop me from disclosing the real truth. The persons who were at the UNDF did not want to accept this reality. In admitting it, I became the target of their vexation because I was a potential enemy, and you deal with an enemy viciously. I must tell you that, for almost three months, I went without any conversation or communication with my family. And I had to bear abuse, and my food was even thrown into the garbage dump. But I did not come before the Tribunal for material reasons, but moral ones. I consider that pleading guilty is a moral cause, and the best that I can do.

To all members of the families of Rwandan victims of 1994; I plead with them to understand that I greatly and sincerely regret what happened in 1994. I plead with them to accept my regret. I know there is nothing I can do, nothing else I can do, but to testify and to bring the horrible truth to light. But I am ready to do this, to make amends or to amend the mistakes that were made. And I plead with them once again to forgive me. ❏

Belgian-born journalist **Georges Ruggiu**, *who worked for Radio-Television Libre des Mille Collines in 1994, was jailed for 12 years on 16 May after pleading guilty to inciting genocide before the UN International Criminal Tribunal for Rwanda* had been freed only ten days earlier. Filipovic wrote a series of exposés for the London-based Institute for War and Peace Reporting that had put the core of the rump Yugoslav government, its military and security services in the spotlight. Filipovic's lawyers have been banned from speaking about the case. (RFE/RL, Institute of War and Peace Reporting)

All universities were ordered to close a week early on 25 May, on the eve of a planned student strike against President Milosevic. Students were permitted to go to class on the day of their exams, but were not able to use the libraries. The decree reflected the regime's concern with the growing influence of the Otpor (resistance) student movement, which has a broad membership but no highly visible leadership. (RFE/RL, *Guardian*, Free B92)

On 8 May **Gillian Sandford**, a freelancer for the *Guardian*, **Natasa Bogovic** and **Bojan Toncic** of the Belgrade independent daily *Danas* and **Mile Veljkovic**, a correspondent from the independent Beta news agency and independent daily *Blic* were detained in Pozarevac while covering an opposition rally. Pozarevac is the home town of President Slobodan Milosevic. (WAN)

Satirist **Boban 'Bapsi' Miletic** was sentenced to five months in jail on 9 June for defamation of the republic and President Milosovic. The judge said he had not been on trial for publishing his book, *Cry, Mother*, which contains aphorisms that 'allegedly

injured the reputation of Slobodan Milosevic'. He was on trial for declaiming aphorisms to a hall full of people at the Knjazevac literary event held in the city's cultural centre on 18 December 1998. (Greek Helsinki Monitor)

It was reported on 17 May that UN officials are investigating the role played by an article in the Albanian-language daily *Dita* on the subsequent murder of **Petar Topljski**, a Serbian working with the UN in Prishtina. The article, which alleged that Topoljski had committed atrocities against Kosovars while fighting as a paramilitary during the 1999 conflict, gave out his address and daily itinerary. An unnamed UN official claimed that the article was tantamount to signing his death warrant. *Dita* was subsequently banned for several days. (RFE/RL)

SOLOMON ISLANDS

It was reported on 4 May – the day after World Press Freedom Day – that the Media Association of the Solomon Islands had helped nine journalists defy a government ban on visits to the conflict area by chartering a plane to fly them to Guadalcanal. (PINA)

SLOVAKIA

Journalist **Vladimir Mohorita**, correspondent for the weekly *Zema*, was sentenced to four months in prison on 7 March under Article 102 for 'publicly defaming the country and its officials'. The charge was brought by Deputy Prime Minister Pal

Czaky, who alleged that an article in the March 1999 edition criticised the government's decision to allow NATO planes to cross Slovak airspace during the Kosovo crisis of 1999. Mohorita filed an official appeal to the Bratislave 2 Regional court, claiming that the court had misquoted his original article. His sentence has been suspended pending the appeal. (WAN)

SPAIN

Jose Luis Lopez de la Calle, a columnist for the pro-government daily *El Mundo*, was killed instantly after being shot four times by an ETA assassin outside his house on 7 May. The Basque separatist group has carried out three violent attacks on Spanish reporters in the past two months. Two journalists received parcel bombs that were safely disarmed by police, while on 21 March a bomb exploded at the home of **Pedro Bringo**, correspondent with the daily *El Correo*. (*International Herald Tribune*)

SRI LANKA

On 6 April **Elmo Fernando**, local correspondent for the BBC's Sinhala-language service, was attacked and injured in front of the Norwegian embassy in Colombo by a group of people protesting against Norway's attempts to facilitate a peace agreement between the government and the separatist Liberation Tigers of Tamil Eelam (LLTE). (CPJ, Free Media Movement)

On 3 May the government put

● ●

MIROSLAV FILIPOVIC
Serb officers relive killings

War-weary Serb officers have spoken for the first time of the atrocities committed by the Yugoslav army in Kosovo during the NATO bombing campaign.

One field commander admitted he watched in horror as a soldier decapitated a three-year-old boy in front of his family. Another described how tanks in his unit indiscriminately shelled Albanian villages before paramilitary police moved in and massacred the survivors.

The confessions were made by officers who took part in a survey commissioned by the Army Intelligence Unit in January and February this year. Particularly disturbing are the combined testimonies of field officers, which suggest that army units were responsible for the deaths of at least 800 Albanian children below the age of five.

One officer, Drazen, said, 'I watched with my own eyes as a reservist lined up around 30 Albanian women and children against a wall. I thought he just wanted to frighten them, but then he crouched down behind an anti-aircraft machine-gun and pulled the trigger. The half-inch bullets just tore their bodies apart. It looked like a scene from a cheap movie, but it really happened.'

Drazen concluded, 'I don't know how I will live with these memories, how I'll be able to raise my own children. I'm not willing to accept the collective guilt. I want to see those who committed these atrocities stand trial for their crimes.'

A reconnaissance officer for an engineering brigade said Yugoslav army reservists in Kosovo ran amok while their commanders did little to intervene. 'The Albanians were standing in a long line along the road leading out of the settlement. A reservist nicknamed Crni (Black) went up to an old man who was holding a child aged around three or four. He grabbed the toddler from the man's arms and demanded a ransom of DM20,000 (US$10,000). The Albanian only had DM5,000. Crni took the child by the hair, pulled out a knife and hacked off its head.'

'Five thousand is only enough for the body,' he said and walked off carrying the child's head by its hair.' ❏

A military court in Nis ordered the rearrest of **Miroslav Filipovic** *on 22 May for 'espionage' and 'spreading false information' as a result of articles he wrote for the independent daily* Danas *and the London-based* Institute for War and Peace Reporting

● ●

the country on a 'war footing' by issuing a 101-page gazette notification under the Public Security Act that said that any events, publications or meetings deemed to threaten national security would be banned. The government has widened its censorship regulations (*Index* 4/1998, 1/2000) to include all war-related news, as well as news and comments on the government and president generally. The new measures follow the loss of the vital Elephant Pass army base to the LTTE on 22 April and amid fears that the Tigers would retake Jaffna Town. (Free Media Movement, Article 19, RSF, Editor Guild of Sri Lanka, *Sunday Times*, *Guardian*, *International Herald Tribune*)

On 11 May the state-run Sri Lanka Broadcasting Corporation (SLBC) took the BBC's Sinhala and Tamil language news programmes off the air. On the same day, BBC and CNN reports broadcast during the news programme of the SLBC's Channel One were blocked by the word 'Censored'. (RSF)

On 15 May the Supreme Court ruled that the present censorship on military news is not a violation of fundamental rights. The decision was made by three judges on a petition filed by **Sunila Abeysekera** of Inform on behalf of a large number of non-governmental organisations. (Associated Press)

Journalists were told on 17 May that they would be barred from covering the special sessions of parliament which will be held

every week to discuss the military situation in the north and east of the country. (Associated Press)

On 17 May the private Telshan Network Limited (TNL), owned by the brother of opposition leader Ranil Wickremasinghe, was threatened with closure after an alleged violation of the censorship regulations. It had transmitted news about a bombing in the eastern town of Batticaloa, in which at least 23 people were killed. (CPJ)

On 19 May the offices of *Uthayan*, the only Tamil-language daily in the northern city of Jaffna, were closed by the government on the grounds that the newspaper had been 'acting maliciously and detrimentally in publishing information that is biased to the LTTE'. (CPJ, *The Times*, Free Media Movement)

The *Sunday Leader* and its Sinhala-language counterpart *Irida Peramuna* were closed for six months when police took over a printing facility operated by Leader Publications Ltd on 22 May. The raid was prompted by a 21 May article in the *Leader*, entitled 'War in Fantasyland', which lampooned the government's censorship policy. (Asian Human Rights Commission, Free Media Movement, *The Times*, *Hindustan Times*, CPJ, RSF)

Ten national newspaper editors went to the Supreme Court on 2 June to accuse Ariya Rubasinghe, the Competent Authority, of enforcing censorship in a selective, subjective and arbitrary manner. They claim that

Rubasinghe is arbitrarily censoring articles, statements and cartoons which do not contain material prejudicial to national security or public order. (*Sunday Times*)

On 3 June the lives of four prominent journalists were threatened when the Independent Television Networks's evening news programme quoted a spurious media organisation called Deshabaktha Madhiya Vijayapara, which branded the men as 'national traitors'. **P. Seevagan**, Secretary of the Sri Lanka Tamil Media Alliance and a freelancer for the BBC Tamil-language service, **Saman Wagaarachchi**, editor of the banned *Irida Peramuna*, **D. Sivaram** (aka Taraki), a senior defence and political affairs columnist, and **Roy Denish**, defence correspondent for the banned *Sunday Leader* and correspondent for *India Today* and *Lanka Academic*, currently fear for their lives. (BBC World Service)

SUDAN

Copies of *Alwan*, *Al Rai*, *Alkher* and *Al Sahafi Ad-Dawli* in Khartoum were seized in early May, allegedly while preparing to publish press releases by the ruling party's deposed general secretary **Hassan al-Tourabi**. The editors-in-chief were summoned on 6 May after receiving a warning from the minister of information regarding the state of emergency which has been in effect since 6 December 1999. (RSF)

SWITZERLAND

The editor and publisher of the white supremacist *Courier du Continent*, **Gaston Armand Amaudruz**, was jailed for one year on 10 April for denying that six million Jews were murdered in the Holocaust. In March 1995 Amaudruz, 79, wrote that the Holocaust was based on 'mythical facts' and, in July of the same year, he published an article entitled '*I Don't Believe the Gas Chambers Existed*'. Judge Michael Carrard said the court had jailed him 'despite his advanced age' because he was one of the 'chief ideologues of the shadowy Far Right'. (*The Times*)

SYRIA

Writer and freelance journalist **Salama George Kayla** was released on 21 March after the expiry of his eight-year sentence. (PEN)

The World Association of Newspapers awarded its annual press freedom prize, the 2000 Golden Pen of Freedom, to imprisoned journalist **Nizar Nayouf** (*Index* 6/1992, 8/1992, 10/1992, 10/1993, 6/1994, 6/1995, 5/1996, 3/1997, 1/1999, 4/1999) in recognition of 'his outstanding services to the cause of press freedom'. (WAN)

TAJIKISTAN

Tajik State TV and Radio Chairman **Saifullo Rakhimov** was shot dead as he returned home from work in Dushanbe on 20 May. Six unidentified attackers blocked his car as it neared his home and opened fire with a sub-

machine gun. President Imomali Rakhmonov condemned the shooting as 'a terrorist act.' On 7 June, relatives of **Abdujabor Sayfulloev**, Rakhimov's driver, identified his body in a Dushanbe morgue. The cause of death has not been disclosed. Sayfulloev was the only known witness to the 20 May attack. (RFE/RL, Reuters, WAN)

TANZANIA

Former opposition member of parliament Stephan Wassira, who allegedly attacked the managing editor of *Hoja* newspaper, **Yasin Rwiza Sadiki**, with a stick is to be charged. The case against Wassira stemmed from an incident on 6 August 1999 when Wassira allegedly beat Sadiki at a Dar-es Salaam conference after being called the Swahili term *swahiba*, interpreted to mean 'gay'. (MISA)

Three Muslim activists – **Seikh Athumani Mussa, Odo Mrisho** and **Ramadhani Rashid** – were arrested in Kigoma on 25 May for possessing 75 audio cassettes, containing speeches against government leaders and other religions. The cassettes were thought to contain material exhorting voters not to elect Christians in the general elections in October. (MISA)

THAILAND

On 18 April **Amnat Khunyosying**, the owner and editor of the Thai-language newspaper *Phak Nua Raiwan* (Northern Daily), was followed by three men in a car as he made his way to the Lanna View

housing estate. The three men shot Khunyosying in the stomach, kicked him and left him for dead. He was rescued by neighbours and taken to McCormick Hospital. According to the *Bangkok Post*, police suspect that the assassination attempt was in retaliation for the paper's aggressive coverage of local political corruption. (CPJ, WAN)

TOGO

Officers of the general information office confiscated all copies of weekly newspaper *L'Exilé* on 13 April. The following day, police arrested and charged the director of the paper **Hippolyte Agboh** with publishing false information after it reported that the president's daughter had died in a car accident. (WAN)

TUNISIA

On 26 April journalist **Taoufik Ben Brick** restarted his hunger strike one day after he halted it because of medical concern over his health (*Index* 4/1999, 2/2000, 3/2000). The decision stemmed from the police's detention and alleged torture of **Ali Ben Salem, Sihem Ben Sedrine** and **Jalal Zouglami**, three activists with unregistered human rights monitoring group Conseil National pour les Libertés en Tunisie, following Ben Brick's decision to end his hunger strike. On 1 May the government returned Ben Brick's confiscated passport, allowing him to travel to Paris for hospitalisation. On 3 May Zouglami was sentenced to a three-month jail term for 'verbally abusing' the police officer responsible for beating Ben Salem. (HRW, CPJ, RSF)

On 2 May journalist **Nureddine Aouididi**, former editor-in-chief of the *Al-Akhabr* newspaper, went on hunger strike over the authorities' refusal to grant her sister Radhia Aouididi a passport to travel to France to join her husband. (IPI)

On 23 May **Raid Ben Fadhel**, former editor of the Arabic-language version of the French monthly *Le Monde Diplomatique*, was seriously injured after unknown gunmen shot two bullets at his chest outside his home in the suburbs of Carthage. The murder attempt is presumably linked to an article published in daily *Le Monde*, headlined 'Let us get rid of the Carthage syndrome' on 21 May, in which he had criticised the handling of the Ben Brick affair by the authorities and warned against amending the constitution to allow President Zine Al-abdine Ben Ali a fourth term in office. The official press suggested he had shot himself. (RSF)

TURKEY

Kemal Onar, an employee of the Batman office of the journal *Ozgur Halk* (Free People) was arrested on 7 April while distributing the paper. He was jailed for 'activities on behalf of the PKK'. (Kurdistan Observer)

The newspaper *Ozgur Bakis*, launched a year ago, was closed down on 22 April. Ninety-seven trials against three editors-in-chief are currently under way and

an Istanbul court had issued investigations in connection with 124 out of the daily's 370 issues (*Index* 5/1999, 1/2000). (*Ozgur Bakis*, Info-Turk)

Following the banning of Kurdish humour magazine *Pine* on 24 April, several newspapers and magazines were prohibited from distributing in the State of Emergency Region. The authorities sent a note to *Ozgur Halk* (Free People), *Yasamda Genclik* (Youth in Life), *Ozgur Kadinin Sesi* (Voice of The Free Woman) and *Rewshen* (The Intellectual), informing them that their sale and distribution was banned in five eastern provinces. (WAN)

Seydi Battal Kose, a police officer who appealed against his sentence for the murder of journalist **Metin Goktepe** (*Index* 2/1996, 6/1996, 1/1997, 6/1997, 1/1998, 2/1998, 3/1998, 5/1998, 1/1999, 2/1999, 4/1999), had his seven-and-a-half year prison term reduced on appeal at the Supreme Court in April to 20 months' imprisonment, a derisory fine and a five-month suspension from duty. Metin's mother and solicitors will appeal. (Campaign for Human Rights in Turkey)

Police raided the Batman office of the Kurdish newspaper *Azadiya Welat* (Freedom of the Homeland) on 4 May and seized the archive. Two of the paper's staff, **Orhan Ekinci** and **Ruken Ekinci**, were detained. (TIHV, Info-Turk)

The editor and a columnist for *Evrensel* newspaper were

summoned to the state prosecutor's office in April to defend statements made in the newspaper. Editor **Fatih Polat** had criticised the militarism and lack of democracy in Turkey, while **Cagdas Gunerbuyuk** was questioned over his criticisms of the military. They were charged with 'belittling the Turkish Armed Forces'. (Campaign for Human Rights in Turkey)

Exiled Kurdish writer **Mahmut Baksi** went on hunger strike on 7 May to protest against the suppression of the Kurdish language and the banning of his two most recent books in south-east Turkey. The author, who is in exile in Sweden, called off his protest after five days with an appearance on Sweden's Channel Four television alongside a government representative. In one of his banned books, entitled *Each bird has its own way of flying*, Baksi attacks the 'political inhumanity of Turkey' with regard to the Kurds. (*Ozgur Politika*)

A newspaper owner was sentenced on 9 May to two years' imprisonment. **Mehmet Kutular**, owner of the daily *Yeni Asir*, was charged with 'inciting people to hatred and enmity'. (*Hurriyet*)

Neriman Sasmaz and **Sahin Seker**, distributors of *Atilim* (*Index* 6/1995, 3/1996), were detained while distributing the newspaper in Istanbul on 10 May and beaten up at Esenkent police station. The two had been charged with resisting the police. Another distributor for the daily *Evrensel* (*Index* 3/1996, 4/1996),

Muzaffer Altinas, was attacked by police and beaten up when he was out distributing the paper. (*Evrensel*, Info-Turk)

It was reported on 12 May that Istanbul Penal Court had confiscated the second edition of the book *Nickname: Hezbollah, The Story of the Turkish Branch of Hezbollah* by journalist **Mehmet Farac** and writer **Faik Bulut** (*Index* 5/1999), on the grounds that it 'insulted the Republic and security forces'. (*Cumhuriyet*)

On 17 May a prosecutor demanded prison terms of up to 15 years for 16 people, including two movie stars and a musician, for publishing a collection of previously banned articles. Musician **Sanar Yurdatan** (*Index* 5/1996, 6/1996, 3/1997, 3/1998, 6/1998, 2/1999, 1/2000, 2/2000) and his sister **Lale Mansur**, a well-known actress, joined 21 other human rights activists and intellectuals in publishing 'Freedom of Thought 2000' (*Index* 6/1996, 5/1998) to protest against the anti-terrorism and anti-sedition laws. (*Turkish Probe*)

Kurdish journal *Zirpine* was restricted from being distributed on the first day of its publication, it was reported on 23 May. The governor of the State of Emergency region imposed the ban on the new publication and effectively stopped it from being distributed. (*Ozgur Politika*)

On 1 June a court in Antep stopped the publication of the local newspaper *Firat'ta Yasam* (Life in Firat) because it had published an article entitled 'Ne

bahari bire min, aclik var' (There is No Spring, My Brother, There is Hunger) – which included the Kurdish phrase 'bire min' (my brother). (*Yeni Gundem*)

Guler Yildiz, editor-in-chief of the weekly *Cinar*, was charged on 26 June with 'insulting the army and the state'. She is accused of having discussed the work of journalist **Nadire Mater** in her newspaper's columns (*Index* 6/1999). (RSF)

TURKMENISTAN

Security police have located **Vitalii Tereshin**, the last remaining Russian Baptist missionary in the country, and deported him, it was reported on 23 May. (Keston News Service)

The Communications Ministry rescinded the licences of all private Internet and email providers on 29 May, claimed applications by the companies had numerous faults. The action leaves state-owned Turkmentelekom as the country's sole provider. (www.ecostan.org, RFE/RL, Interfax, Reuters)

UGANDA

Newscaster **Frank Bangonza Kimoone** and reporter **Joseph Kasimbazi** of the community radio station Voice of Tororo were detained on 16-17 February in connection with a 15 February broadcast alleging that three dozen civilians from Kijura, a village near Fort Portal, had been massacred the previous night by rebels of the Allied Democratic forces (ADF). The two journalists were held in a small cell for one

week. According to Ugandan journalists, Kasimbazi learned of the alleged massacre from a Kijura village leader and Kimoone read his report on air quoting 'unconfirmed reports'. An hour later, it became clear that no such thing had happened. Voice of Tororo aired a correction and apology in English and several local dialects. Kimoone and Kasimbazi appeared before the courts charged with 'sedition and publication of false and alarmist news' and released on US$170 bail each, pending further investigations. (CPJ)

UKRAINE

Jed Sunden, publisher of the independent *Kyiv Post*, has been prohibited from entering the country in which he has lived for several years, it was reported on 11 April. Sunden was returning to his Kiev residence from Turkey when he was detained by border police at Borispil international airport and told he was denied entry for one year. *Kyiv Pos* has regularly published articles critical of corruption, bureaucracy and the slow pace of reform. (WAN)

Editor-in-chief of the weekly *Svoboda* (formerly *Politika*) **Oleg Liachko** was assaulted and beaten after the publication of an article on 13 March that alleged a series of links between Yuri Kulbachenko, a deputy on Odessa town council, state security agencies and local criminal organisations. On 31 March Kulbachenko invited Liachko to a meeting in Kiev and ordered him to reveal his sources. When Liachko refused he was attacked by the politician and suffered concussion. The police file investigating the beating was closed on 6 April with no explanation. (CPJ)

USA

A reporter for the *Wichita Eagle* in Kansas was forced to hand over all material from an interview done with a murder suspect. **Tanner Green**, suspected of the brutal murder of Janice Vredenburg, made a call to reporter **Tim Potter** and they spoke for an hour and a half. He had previously refused to talk to police about the murder. The *Eagle* published its story on 19 April and received subpoenas the next day. Editor **Rick Thomas** did not appeal because Kansas, unlike 31 other states, has no 'shield law' to prevent government agencies from seizing files from the press. (Freedom Forun)

Louis Farrakhan admitted that he 'may have been complicit in words' in the 1965 assassination of his rival **Malcolm X**. He admits that what he wrote and spoke in December 1964 might have inspired the shooting, it was reported on 12 May. He had written about Malcolm X: 'Such a man is worthy of death', after Malcolm X criticised the Nation of Islam's spiritual leader, Elijah Muhammad. (*The Times*)

VENEZUELA

Hundreds of journalists marched through Caracas on 4 May to protest against the abuses allegedly committed by President Hugo Chávez against the press. Led by the Workers Press Union,

demonstrators also showed solidarity with journalist and TV producer **Napoleón Bravo**, whose programme was shut down allegedly as a result of government pressure. (IFJ)

VIETNAM

Sylvaine Pasquire, a journalist with the French weekly *L'Express*, was forced to leave the country after being arrested on 13 April. Pasquire was covering the 25th anniversary of the fall of Saigon but had tried to meet dissidents. (RSF)

On 30 April journalist and dissident Nguyen Ngoc Tan, known as **Pham Thai**, was freed six years before the end of his sentence. Pham Thai, 80, was allegedly released from the Ham Tan work camp on humanitarian grounds. He had worked as a journalist with the Movement for the Unity of the People and Construction of Democracy and in 1995 was sentenced to 11 years in prison for 'conspiring against the socialist power'. (RSF)

On 12 May pro-democracy activist **Ha Si Phu** was placed under house arrest in Lam Dong province by police, who threatened to charge him with treason. If convicted Ha could face a sentence from seven years' imprisonment to the death penalty. A biologist and former vice-director of the Vietnamese Institute of Science, Ha is suspected of being connected to the drafters of an open appeal for greater democracy in Vietnam. (HRW)

YEMEN

On 10 May the Seera Court of First Instance charged **Hisham Basharaheel**, editor-in-chief and publisher of the independent thrice-weekly newspaper *Al-Ayyam*, with publishing 'false information', 'instigating the use of force and terrorism' and insulting 'public institutions'. The charges stem from an interview in *Al-Ayyam* with London-based Muslim cleric **Abu Hamza al-Masri**. If convicted, Basaraheel faces up to three years imprisonment and fines. Last August he was sentenced to six months' suspended sentence for 'instigating national feuds' (*Index* 5/1999). (CPJ)

On 24 May Criminal Investigation officers detained **Khalid Al-Hamadi**, correspondent of the London-based *Al-Quds Al-Arabi* newspaper. Officers forcibly took his camera and destroyed it, along with the film. (*Yemeni Bulletin*)

Arafat Muddabish, correspondent of the United Arab Emirates' *Al-Itihad* newpaper and the local *Al-Ayyam*, was brutally beaten by policemen on 29 May outside the appeal court as he tried to take pictures of Mohammed Adem Omar, the morgue assistant at Sana'a University, who was standing trial for raping 16 girls. Arafat suffered serious injuries and was rushed to the hospital for treatment. (*Yemeni Bulletin*)

ZIMBABWE

On 22 April a home-made bomb was hurled at the entrance of

Harare-based independent *Daily News*. The bomb caused no injuries and little damage, but was the latest incident in a campaign of harassment. In the weeks preceding, editor-in-chief **Geoff Nyarota** received death threats in the mail from a group identifying itself as the Restoration of African Conscience. The group accused the paper of biased reported and threatened to 'do away with' Nyarota. Information Minister Chenhamo Chimutengwende accused the *Daily News* of orchestrating the bombing itself to tarnish the country's international reputation. (CPJ)

AAP journalist **Obed Zilwa** appeared in court on 2-3 May to answer charges that he was involved in the 22 April bombing of the *Daily News* offices. Zilwa, a South African, had been covering the land dispute in Harare when he was arrested and interrogated by security forces for seven hours on 26 April. As well as questioning him about his involvement in the bombing, officers asked Zilwa whether or not he supported the farm invasions. Zilwa was one of the first journalists to arrive at the scene of the bombing, as his hotel was a few blocks away. Police say Zilwa matches the description of the suspect who was seen speeding from the scene. (Freedom of Expression Institute, CPJ, MISA)

The independent Media Monitoring Project Zimbabwe (MMPZ) concluded that 'the state-controlled media have … abandoned all pretence at providing their readers, viewers and listeners with balanced or fair coverage of election issues', it was reported on 17 May. (MMPZ)

The Supreme Court dismisssed all charges against reporters **Mark Chavandunka** and **Ray Choto** (*Index* 3/1999, 2/2000, 3/2000) on 22 May, saying the legislation under which the two *Standard* journalists were charged was 'too unclear' to uphold earlier judgements in the lower courts. Chavandunka and Choto were arrested on 12 and 14 January 1999 respectively and charged with publishing false information 'likely to cause fear and despondency'. The pair have filed criminal and civil charges against the police for wrongful arrest, detention, assault and torture. (CPJ)

On 6 June the chairman of the Zimbabwe National Liberation War Veterans Association, Chenjerai Hunzvi, issued a public warning to the *Daily News* to desist from publishing articles that he claims tarnishes his reputation. Editor-in-chief **Geoff Nyarota** said the paper did not publish for the pleasure of any individual, but for the benefit of its readers. (MISA)

It was reported on 9 June that copies of the *Zimbabwe Independent*, the *Standard* and *Daily News* were continuously stolen from vendors and burned by supporters of the war veterans and members of ZANU-PF, who claimed during the ransackings that the papers 'misinformed' people. (MISA)

Compiled by: Melanie Clark, Shifa Rahman, Daniel Rogers (Africa); Ben Carrdus, Rupert Clayton, Heidi Joyce, Andrew Kendle (Asia); William Escofet, Daniel Rogers (south and central America); Arif Azad, Gill Newsham, Neil Sammonds (Middle East); Humfrey Hunter (north America and Pacific); Deborah Haynes (Britain and western Europe); Katy Sheppard (eastern Europe and the Balkans).

Australian rules

Australia has seen more censorship laws passed in four years of John Howard's government than ever before in its history. This tide has washed away the entitlement of Aborigines to their land and languages, immigrants, journalists, Web-users – and the one-in-four Australians who consume pornography

File compiled by Phillip Adams

DAVID MARR

Suspect pleasure

Terrible things can happen in Australia, but this is one of the safest, most peaceful countries on earth. Politicians prosper here by talking up crime and blaming these horrors on the screen, the Internet, video and television. Their audience is familiar anywhere in the western world: disgruntled conservatives who expect 'protection' for themselves and their children and are willing to change political sides to get it. They aren't typical, but they swing elections.

The genius of John Howard was to bring these people under his wing. They don't like Aborigines, they're loyal to Queen Elizabeth, they're stand-offish about Asia – and particularly fearful of what might be brought into their homes by cable, video and the Internet. Howard knows them because he's one of them and, in 1996, they made him prime minister. Censorship has been tightening ever since and only lately has the need to resist it become a political issue. It's not one the Labor opposition is running with: they want these disgruntled voters too. Labor has blessed most of what John Howard's government has done.

Censorship in Australia is a tale of contradictions. This is a country strongly committed to freedom of choice for adults to see and read what they choose – the porn industry conducts professional polling to remind politicians (fruitlessly) of this – but all political parties are happy to trade that freedom away for crucial votes. We're also one of the most secular countries on earth, but churches are the key players in this.

We inherited a tough strain of Christianity in the Antipodes. From the moment the first priest and missionaries were rowed ashore at Sydney Cove, watched by assembled felons and savages at the edge of the bush, men of God here have seen themselves as ministering to human beings at their worst. And the work is particularly urgent because of their reasonable fear that God's mission in Australia can so easily be sabotaged by pleasure – by sun, sex, sea and overwhelming prosperity. The churches in Australia love authority, suspect pleasure and lobby hard.

Another contradiction: calls for censorship are all the more effective these days because the traditional social agenda of the Church – concern for fairness, for the poor, the marginalised and the immigrant – doesn't have a hope in John Howard's Australia. The hostility of modern politics to that agenda leaves Christians weaker in pressing for social equity – but all the stronger in calls for censorship. Less flesh on television and cops to police the Internet are consolation prizes easily awarded to a lobby that's never going to stop harassing government, nor be given what it really wants: a fair society.

So society's key disgruntled voters are being enrolled in crusades against sex and women and homosexuals; in the harassment of AIDS and HIV-prevention programmes; in the ruthless 'War on Drugs'; and in the persecution of erotic books, films, paintings and video. This goes on all round the world and has, in one way or another, from the beginning of time. But right now in Australia, governments are listening. ❏

David Marr *is a writer and president of Australia's Watch on Censorship. His most recent book,* The High Price of Heaven, *is about the malign impact of religious belief on Australian politics. He is the biographer of novelist Patrick White*

PHILLIP ADAMS

Wowsers on parade

Hot on the heels of the Olympics, a collection of states and bigotries, territories and ideals, will try to celebrate the Australian centenary

A hundred years ago, a scattering of separate colonies agreed to federate. A serviceable, matter-of-fact constitution was hammered out, devoid of rhetorical flourish. Freedom of speech wasn't guaranteed, there was no First Amendment and the founding fathers declined to provide us with a Bill of Rights. In recent years, an interventionist High Court has held the document to the light and, through judicial squinting, discovered a hint of guaranteed liberties. So much so that they've taken to mentioning 'free speech' in certain decisions.

That the new nation was conceived with more wariness than enthusiasm was dramatised by a lack of agreement on one of the most basic issues: a common railway gauge. North and south, east and west, never the trains should meet. Or they could, but passengers and freight had to be shifted into new rolling stock, or have replacement bogeys fitted. The states did manage to get on the right track in regard to the straight and narrow subject of censorship. It would be draconian. It would be silly. And occasional outbursts of reforming zeal would be countered by backlashes organised by generation after generation of wowsers.

Censorship began with concerns about literature, the visual arts and, further down the tracks, cinema. Australia has long censored its past, particularly with regard to people who didn't meet the British standards of skin colour that Australia inherited. If you didn't accord to the Greenwich Mean of pinkness, you'd be drummed from the regiment. Or you wouldn't be allowed to volunteer. While proud of its new identity, Australia remained resolutely Anglophile and continued to prove its transplanted patriotism by haring off to fight British wars. Having chased the Boers over the veld (and there's a rumour that some Australians fought in the Crimean War), we sacrificed an entire generation on Britain's behalf at Gallipoli. Given a silly strategy by Churchill and a commander like Sir Ian Hamilton, our grandfathers couldn't wait to be mowed down. Curiously, it was Rupert Murdoch's war correspondent father, Keith Murdoch, who condemned the Gallipoli operation with such intensity that Hamilton lost his command. He left it to his son to punish you pommy bastards with a one-man invasion of Fleet Street.

On Federation Day, 1 January 1901, we decided to censor anyone who wasn't British. We introduced the White Australia Policy to censor the overwhelming majority of the world's population. Asians and Indians would find the welcome mat replaced by a portcullis and, with the exception of indentured labour imported to cut Queensland's sugar cane, blacks were far, far beyond the pale. Even worse was the great silence that descended on our indigenous population, regarded as 'doomed' by the Protestant Ascendancy in control of Australia, which decided to ignore them as much as inhumanly possible. Divested of their lands, Aborigines would be stripped of citizenship and human rights. They were censored from the census. No Aborigine would be counted for almost 70 years.

Australia's customs service was the only branch of public service in which Roman Catholics could expect promotion. Officers searched incoming luggage with commendable zeal, in the hope of finding DH Lawrence's *Lady Chatterley's Lover*, Mary McCarthy's *The Group*, Vladimir Nabokov's *Lolita* and Hugh Hefner's *Playboy*. The vice squad entered Melbourne's most famous emporium to arrest a life-size replica of Michelangelo's David on charges of gross public indecency. Simultaneously, their colleagues, known as 'Lily Law', loitered in toilets in the hope of arresting consenting adults.

Film censorship was particularly zealous, with even festivals being filleted of anything regarded as salacious. I made a three-hour documentary on Australia's sexual mores called *The Naked Bunyip* (the bunyip being a mythical creature that lurks in water holes, a sort of hybrid of cow and goanna). The chief censor took to the production with zeal, hacking out references to lesbianism and deleting any follicles of pubic hair. I protested, pointing out that foreign films on lesbianism were screening at art cinemas in Melbourne and in Sydney. 'They're foreigners,' the chief censor told me, 'I will not tolerate Australian nudity or Australian lesbianism.' He removed almost 30 minutes from our three-hour film – and was aghast when we retaliated by refusing to mend the wreckage. Instead, we had an animated bunyip cavort on the screen for the duration of every cut, accompanied with flashing lights and the sound of police sirens. The 'cuts' proved the most popular part of the film.

Having accumulated vast hangars full of soft porn and high literature, customs officials were told in the late 1960s to turn a blind eye to moral turpitude. Australia laid down its heavy burden of censorship with such relief that, for a time, there was dancing in the street. All sorts of human activities escaped the wowsers and the vice squad: abortion, prostitution, gambling and, in some states, homosexual acts between consenting adults. All these activities had continued despite legislative caveats because prohibition had made police and political corruption inevitable, as does the policy of censoring and demonising narcotics half a century later.

More significantly, the Australia of the late 1960s and early 1970s decided to stop censoring non-whites. Responding to international embarrassment, economic reality and a disturbing growth in progressive opinion, Canberra decided it was time to scrap White Australia. Australians who'd been rude to Italians and Greeks learned to enjoy cappuccino and dolmades. It even began to consider the possibility that Aborigines might be important to Australia's history, culture and well-being.

For a while we rejoiced in tolerance, we wallowed in it. I was appointed to the Council of Australian Governments committee, representing federal, state and territorial authorities, to report on how Australia should celebrate its hundredth birthday. We toured the country taking submissions from organisations and individuals. I always asked people to tell us what made them proud to be Australian. It was tolerance, tolerance, tolerance. It became a chant, a litany, a central tenet. Forgetting that Australia was born in intolerance and had maintained that tradition proudly for 70 years, we now saw ourselves as representing world's best practice. Tolerance was as central to our psyche as eucalyptus, kangaroos and Test cricket.

Our final report took Australians at their word. We described 2001 as our coming of age, the time when we'd be able to display our tolerant, multicultural nation to the world. On 1 January 2001 we imagined Australia becoming a republic and, more important, having at the very least a ceremonial reconciliation with the indigenous population. But none of it was meant to be. The republic was scuttled by an extraordinarily mendacious conservative campaign and the reconciliation process is in ruins. Four years ago, Australians elected the ultra-conservative John Howard to government in a coalition of his illiberal Liberal Party and a National Party claiming to represent the views of the rural citizen. From the moment Howard swore allegiance to Queen Elizabeth, the clock has been turned back.

During the term of the previous Labor government, in 1992, the High Court decided it was time to stop censoring history. In the so-called Mabo judgment (named for Eddie Mabo, an indigenous person who'd taken a lands-right case to our loftiest judges), the court announced that *terra nullius* had been a fib. *Terra nullius*? The argument that Australia had been, effectively, a land devoid of anyone who could be described as human. In contrast to other British colonies, where the previous occupants had been given enduring rights under treaties, *terra nullius* allowed awesome land grabs to continue ruthlessly for 200 years after white settlement began. The High Court that had detected faint gleams of free speech in the constitution did even better with Mabo. *Terra nullius* was nullified. Under strict circumstances, indigenous people could claim back ancestral lands.

Conservative government in Canberra and the states and territories started responding to – and encouraging – a white backlash. Anxious to tell the true story of indigenous people, progressive historians were denigrated by Prime Minister Howard for pushing a 'black armband' view of history. Not for the first time in his career, he also suggested that Asian immigration might become a problem for a culture based 'first and foremost' on a British heritage.

He told Australians they'd been subjected to a form of censorship called 'political correctness'. This had never gained the head of steam one could observe in US universities, but Howard insisted that PC had stifled healthy debate on issues like Asian immigration and, yes, Aboriginal land rights. Few of us had noticed that our national conversations had been stultified, let alone that our racists and bigots had been bound hand and mouth. Political life had increasingly been dominated by the 'shock-jocks' – loud Australian echoes of the unfortunate US phenomenon – whose views were amplified by pundits in both tabloid and broadsheet press and, with a little help from conservative think-tanks, were well on the way to setting the political agenda. With prime ministerial approval, racism had a field day. Aborigines and Asian immigrants (and Asian tourists) reported a rising incidence of attacks.

The principal symptom of Australian PC had been an attempt by groups representing the ethnic communities – in particular the Jewish community – to have Labor governments, state and federal, introduce laws forbidding racial vilification. As the debate raged, it was suggested that these laws be turbo-charged with criminal sanctions. Which meant that Australians could be sent to jail for saying things, rather than doing things. This was opposed by some among us, though it forced us into unpalatable collaboration with extreme right-wing groups campaigning, for example, to have the government's ban on visits by historian David Irving overturned (*Index* 3/2000). Censorship was suddenly advocated by the left, by people previously identified with progressive attitudes. Suddenly, old warriors of the 1960s, who fought at the barricades, were saying: 'But this wasn't what we fought for.' The speed-up in media, their increasing triviality of news and public affairs, the plummeting ratings for serious radio, the death and dearth of good magazines, the bans on David Irving were other causes for concern.

Coinciding with the election of the Howard government came the One Nation Party, an antipodean echo of the Le Pen movement in France, led by a Pauline Hanson, who was as strident as she was ignorant. Her electoral success, though short-lived, tilted politics to the right as the major parties struggled to appease the bigotries of her followers. At the time of writing, One Nation seems to have destroyed itself with a combination of lunatic leadership and financial scandal – but, to borrow from Waltzing Matilda, its ghost may be heard as you walk by the billabong. Or by Lake Burley Griffin, the man-made stretch of water in front of Parliament House. Many believe that One Nation will rise from its dark waters, like Godzilla from Tokyo Bay, in time for the next federal election.

One Nation's central beliefs have been incorporated into the policies of the mainstream. Just before the last federal election, Barry Jones, then

Pauline Hanson wrapped in the flag – Credit: Rankin/Rex

president of the Australian Labor Party (ALP), told me that voters would have a choice between 'ALP, who'd give the voters 50% of what One Nation wanted, the Liberal Party who'd offer them 70% and the National Party who'd give Hanson's followers 110%'.

Australians, black and white, had been working towards 'reconciliation' in time for the centenary of federation. Many believed that reconciliation would coincide with the new Australian republic, but Prime Minister Howard put paid to the latter and remains unsympathetic to the former. In particular, he has censored the word 'apology', refusing an official *mea culpa* to the Aboriginal communities, particularly in regard to the so-called 'stolen generation'. The policy of removing half-caste children from Aboriginal communities became the focus of a Human Rights Commission report called *Bringing Them Home*. For decades, for generations, a multitude of children had been taken, by force, deception or intimidation, from Aboriginal parents to be trained as domestics and, through this procedure, to become assimilated. Official documents reveal that the policy was, in effect, soft-core genocide – and *Bringing Them Home* told of the tragic consequences.

Howard did his best to distract the electorate. He procrastinated on tabling the report in parliament, then used the old ruse of tabling it during a busy parliamentary period. More seriously, the government sought to discredit Sir Ronald Wilson, previously a High Court judge and chair of the commission. That wasn't enough. When the report generated intense disquiet, the government cut the commission's budget and 'redefined' its terms of reference. There's a new political correctness, a PC of the hard right, that seeks to replace 'black armband' history with white blinkers. It seeks nothing less than the repression of national memory on this issue – just as colonial governments used *terra nullius* to clear the conscience of early settlers.

With the rise of the rural right – and bigotry towards Aborigines rising in the polls – *terra nullius* is alive and well and living in the minds of organisations such as the National Farmers' Federation. Extremists, connected by the Internet to such US institutions as the National Rifle Association, Aryan Nation and the Ku Klux Klan, can be heard murmuring about the virtues of White Australia. And Howard, who boasts of himself as 'the most conservative political leader Australia has ever had', has been muttering pieties about media violence and pornography. His government has been trying (or at least pretending) to prune porn and violence from the Internet – though not the hate pages that encourage racist violence.

Howard has also attempted to belittle the Australian Broadcasting Corporation (ABC), by cutting its budget, stacking its board and finding suitable conservatives to manage the place. In a country where the media is close to an oligopoly, owned by Rupert Murdoch and Kerry Packer, ABC is the only significant independent voice – but attempts to gag it continue on an hourly basis. To be fair, Howard is not the first prime minister to hate the place. Labor's Paul Keating was decidedly hostile and his predecessor, Bob Hawke, never forgave the network for criticising his Desert Storm policy – or for screening the programmes of John Pilger whom he seemed to regard as the anti-Christ.

Meanwhile, even the bravest journalists in commercial media face the most insidious of all forms of censorship – self-censorship. When there are only two potential employers – Rupert or Kerry – it is a brave person who raises issues inimical to a tycoon's interests or attitudes. This is leading to a dulling-down which, in parallel with a dumbing-down, produces an increasingly ill-served reader, listener or viewer. Many major cities have a single newspaper: independent journals, previously influential in politics, have disappeared – and the price of entry for new titles is prohibitive. With ABC and SBS (the multicultural broadcasting service) being progressively marginalised – both organisations were refused additional funding in the recent budget – we face the prospect of being ill-informed in the information age. Optimists are ecstatic about the Internet, of course, but thus far the familiar roll-call of tycoons seems to have things pretty much under control.

For all their sins, neither Rupert nor Kerry can be blamed for the recent scandal, called 'Cash for Comment'. The kerfuffle concerned Australia's most influential talk radio station, Sydney's 2UE, two of whose highest paid broadcasters were discovered to have provided editorial comment and pre-scripted interviews for commercial interests, which paid them millions per annum. After a prolonged inquiry – and devastating judgments on media scruples – everyone's still at it. All they are now required to do is admit that they're being paid for their opinions – confessions that they treat with derision.

So it's two steps forward, one step back. The country that will celebrate its 100th birthday in 2001 bears little relationship to the Australia devised by our founding fathers. They based their notion of nationhood on principles of exclusion, whereas today Australia is exuberantly inclusive. We are made up of as many nationalities, religions, cultures and subcultures as any country on earth. But the armies of the night are on the march and bigotry, like anthrax, can still cause sudden infections in the body politic. And the wowsers, who we thought dead and buried, have regrouped to fight their battles all over again. ❏

Phillip Adams' radio programme 'Late Night Live' *is broadcast twice daily over the 200 stations of Radio National and by Radio Australia. His books include* Adams versus God, Retreat from Tolerance *and* A Billion Voices. *He directed* The Adventures of Barry McKenzie, Don's Party, The Getting of Wisdom, Lonely Hearts *and* We of the Never Never. *He was recently elected one of Australia's 100 National Living Treasures*

TERRY LANE

A SLAPP in time

Strategic Litigation Against Public Participation is Australia's preferred way of dealing with social critics and has become the most serious threat to free speech

A lan Gray is a greenie. He loves forests and wants to keep them as God created them. In April 1999, he planned to publish a book called *Forest Friendly Building Timbers*, a consumer guide to timbers and timber substitutes that are strong, useful and not taken from old-growth native forests. Gray arranged a pre-publication contract with BBC Hardware, a nationwide chain of hardware stores. They paid for a number of advertisements in the book. On the basis of the order, Gray increased his print run; and there were plans to launch the book in BBC's outlets.

Enter the National Association of Forest Industries (NAFI) – 'guild' of the logging industry. NAFI set its lawyers onto Gray and BBC Hardware. The NAFI lawyers claimed that *Forest Friendly Building Timbers* contravened sections 52, 53 and 55 of the Trade Practices Act (TPA) – clauses which prohibit one company from damaging the 'good name' and trading operations of another. They ordered Gray to cease and desist from publication of the book and to pulp all copies forthwith.

NAFI also put pressure on BBC, which reneged on the contract to stock the book, claiming never to have heard of it, in spite of the fact that the book contained four display advertisements for the company. There are serious shenanigans going on here. The big question, however, is this: is the TPA the latest addition to a collection of laws that can be used to censor uncomfortable opinions? Alan Gray was worried. The threats against him were so dire he feared he might lose all his worldly possessions. For the price of a lawyer's letter – a couple of hundred tax-deductible dollars – NAFI had put the fear of bankruptcy into him.

Alan Gray and I were on nodding acquaintance. He was a regular guest on an ABC radio programme for which I broadcast. He asked if Free Speech Victoria could offer him any assistance. My heart sank. On the face of it his cause looked lost because the relevant clauses in the Act forbid a person or company from doing anything that would damage the business of another person or company. There are penalties and costs and damages that can be recovered.

I am blessed with a quick-thinking producer, Peter Browne. He suggested that we invite Professor Allan Fels onto the programme and ask him for his interpretation of the Act. Fels is chairman of the Australian Competition and Consumer Commission, the government office that administers the TPA. Fels rose to the occasion with alacrity. He blew the NAFI case out of the water, pointing to another clause in the Act that specifically exempts critical publications, such as books, magazines and radio broadcasts. He went further, suggesting that Gray had grounds for taking legal action against NAFI for misuse of the Act to intimidate a critic. The tables had been turned and the consequent publicity made *Forest Friendly Building Timbers* a best-seller. Would that all such stories had happy endings.

Again in 1999, a group of residents in the Victorian seaside resort of Lorne protested against the redevelopment of a quaint old guesthouse on the foreshore. The residents didn't want the Gold Coast coming into Lorne so they got together and began a campaign to stop the development. An article praising the development appeared in the *Melbourne Sunday Age*. In response, two Lorne locals wrote to the editor, taking exception to the tone of PR puffery in what purported to be a piece of reportage. The letter writers were immediately hit with a demand that they withdraw all their criticisms and apologise and that they do it in paid advertisements in the next week's edition. If you don't, the lawyer wrote, we have booked the court for next Monday morning. The threat was ridiculous. Lawyers cannot book courts. But it worked. The residents paid for the advertisements of retraction and retired hurt from the fray.

The Lorne story is more typical of the outcomes of these SLAPPs, as they are known, than the Alan Gray case. 'Strategic Litigation Against Public Participation' is now the preferred way of dealing with social critics in Australia. Books are no longer censored by a censorship board. X-rated videos still float around the country. By and large films are more lightly censored in Australia than in Britain, although film and television censorship is erratic and inconsistent. But dare to criticise a profit-driven corporation or individual and you find that censorship is alive and well.

Tim Malseed is an office holder in a suburban branch of the Liberal Party, the Australian equivalent of the Tories. Malseed reckoned that the local free newspaper in his area had a Labor bias. An engineer, and no stranger to statistical analysis, he bought a book on media content analysis and set out to check the bias of the *Diamond Valley News*, a Murdoch newspaper. Malseed counted column inches, multiplied them by advertising rates for that particular page and so on. He produced charts and diagrams and sent them to the news editor of the paper, with copies to Lachlan Murdoch, who runs this part of his father's empire; Senator Richard Alston, the minister for communications; the chairman of the Press Council; and some other perfectly appropriate recipients. What did the news editor of the *Diamond Valley News* do with this information? She sued for defamation.

The case dragged on for months resulting in the waste of a great deal of money and ending in one of those stalemates that frequently occur in these cases, with everyone swearing not to disclose the terms of the settlement. Now if it is not safe to complain of political bias in a newspaper, what can you complain about?

Even the Australian Broadcasting Corporation – for which I work – has tried its hand at censoring a critic. John Bennett, a lawyer with a reputation as a 'historical revisionist', publishes an annual booklet called *Your Rights*. It is mainly a catalogue of advice about what to do when stopped by the cops or when you have a complaint against a neighbour or a government department – legal consumer advice you might call it. But Bennett also uses the booklet to promote some of his less popular opinions, including an ongoing grievance he has with ABC about its complaints handling procedure.

In the 1999 edition of *Your Rights*, Bennett described his attempts to complain to the ABC about the treatment of the eccentric politician Pauline Hanson. Hanson is not popular with the left intelligentsia and gets rough treatment on ABC. But what we think of Hanson or Bennett is not the point. What was printed in his booklet was no more savage than you might expect to read in an average letter to the editor complaining about the high-handedness of the corporation in its dealings with critics.

ABC sent a lawyer's letter to the distributors of the booklet, Gordon and Gotch, ordering them to cease handling *Your Rights* forthwith. It is not clear what law the corporation was relying on for intimidation, but there was enough menace to persuade Gordon and Gotch to drop the book. The distributors lost no time in informing Bennett that they would not be distributing *Your Rights* from fear of some unspecified consequence from the ABC. Intervention by a number of individuals and Free Speech Victoria resulted in ABC backing down, but the disturbing question remains: why did a broadcasting organisation think it could deal with a critic by censoring him?

The Murdoch and ABC cases are extraordinary, suggesting as they do an obsessive urge by two media organisations to control what is said about them, when the whole purpose of their existence is to print and broadcast news which, by definition, is something that someone somewhere doesn't want to be known, or said. Free Speech Victoria believes that the defamation, racial vilification and trade practices laws are now the greatest threats to free speech and the most frequently used instruments of censorship here. We have begun a campaign to have the laws reformed. It will be a long and difficult crusade because politicians are accustomed to regarding defamation settlements as a useful source of income. Last year, two federal ministers walked away from court with settlements in excess of five times the national average wage – and there is no tax to pay, so in effect it was more like eight times the average wage. Indeed politicians defend the present bizarre arrangement in which defamation laws vary from state to state, because it broadens their opportunities for legal action.

Former prime minister Paul Keating was a hard man and quick to take offence, but he had one redeeming quality. He declared that he would never sue a critic for defamation because politicians have to expect to be defamed. Free Speech Victoria wants the Keating principle enshrined in legislation so that the relatively powerless individual citizen may speak up and say what is on his or her mind without fear of losing the house as a consequence of a few words that may be technically libellous, but are in fact no more than fair comment in a free, open and democratic society. Politicians will fight such reform, but the list of affronts to freedom of speech grows longer every day. ❏

Terry Lane is a broadcaster, writer and president of Free Speech Victoria

COLIN TATZ

Uneven playing field

You don't expect to find exclusion and censorship on the playing field, especially in sports-mad Australia. But sport isn't a prophylactic against prejudice

Ten or 11 Aborigines, chosen on merit, will be participating in the Australian national team of around 600 competitiors at the 2000 Olympics. As just on 353,000 people comprise the Aborigines, Torres Strait and South Sea Islanders, the 'indigenous' percentage looks good. It is also promoted *as* good because it serves three purposes: it allows us to sweep away the past by pointing to the pleasant present; gives us a chance to appropriate success, grace, social mobility and respect for Aboriginal athletes as merely part of 'ordinary' collective 'Australian-ness'; and, despite the contradiction, gives us simultaneous licence to herald track athlete Cathy Freeman – *the* national icon – as representative of all Aboriginality, certainly of the whole of Aboriginal womanhood. If only this were so.

Since the end of black American slavery, no other group in history has endured anything like the Aborigines' suffering under the gun and the whip, the neck chains and the rape, the exile to remoteness, the break-up of families, the forcible removal of children, special legislation, indefinite periods of wardship and legal minority status, exclusion from what we call citizenship, and denial of what we understand by civil rights. The past is hardly a foreign country, and the censorship of Aborigines – their being defined in and out of Australian society – hasn't ceased, either on or off the field. Censoring *in* is a fairly recent twist, as I will explain.

Nineteenth-century missionaries – notably the draconian

Benedictines – saw cricket as a civilising activity and introduced it to 'these poor natives ... so hideous to look at'. Christian lips and Christian pens saw them as 'children of Satan', 'vice-hardened', 'loathsome', 'depraved', 'degraded', 'treacherous', 'cruel' and 'miserable'. All-Aboriginal teams enjoyed some cricketing success – including a famous tour to England in 1868 – but cricketing evangelism was short-lived. By the early 1900s, the authorities put a stop to it: 'They had evidently been too much encouraged in competition with Europeans in the way of cricket matches, etc, and had been treated socially far above their natural station in life.' That was the verdict of the first Chief Protector of Aborigines in Queensland, Archibald Meston, whose task was to save Aborigines from the genocidal impulses of the squatters and settlers.

If Aborigines were to use sporting prowess as a means of escaping incarceration on reserves and missions, their only other sporting avenue was professional running, then called 'pedestrianism'. They were very good at it. In the 1880s, Charlie Samuels was king of the tracks. The major sports paper, the *Referee*, declared him the best ever – even though 'it might be a more pleasant reflection to Australians, perhaps, if a white man could be quoted as champion'. Athletes and fans at Fraser Island wrote to the Queensland governor asking that Aborigines be banned from competition – because they always won! The Queensland Amateur Athletic Association excluded Aborigines by the expedient of calling them all professionals. And the professionals listed every black runner's name on the programme with an 'a', a 'cp' or an 'hc' – for 'aboriginal', 'coloured person' or 'half-caste' – lest, it was claimed, 'the public be misled'.

This popular sport died of corruption, to be replaced in the public enthusiasm by an assortment of animal races. The only sporting escape left for Aborigines – now all incarcerated as a legal and geographic race apart in the remotest of reserves – was boxing. Jerry Jerome won the Australian middleweight championship in 1912. Since then, 51 Aboriginal men have won 71 national professional titles and 27 have won 51 national amateur crowns (to the end of 1999). Ring success lay in the ease of access to the game – in that nearly all other sporting avenues were closed – and in the irresistible chance of a quick quid. Over-represented in proportion to their numbers, certainly, but – like most boxers, especially black ones – they were, and are, grossly exploited, mismanaged and treated as a breed of gladiators. Several boxers were encouraged to drink, the sooner to be in need of more fights and more money. In 1946, George Kapeen had 15 ten-round bouts in 60 days – an indictment of all involved.

Despite the negatives, boxing was, until very recently, the glory sport for Aborigines, the way out of the reserve, poverty, indignity. Boxing-tent fighter Henry Collins said it plainly: 'I felt good when I knocked white blokes out. I felt good. I knew I was boss in the boxing ring. I showed my superiority … they showed it outside.' If not quite dead, boxing is terminally ill – which perhaps explains why so many Aborigines have remained amateurs. Two of Australia's ten Olympic boxers for Sydney are Aborigines from the Northern Territory.

Australian football and rugby league now boast an over-representation of Aboriginal players: something like ten to 13% of senior division players, yet they are a bare two per cent of the population. Does this reflect a change for the better? Yes. But are such percentages a sleight of historical hand, a way of obfuscating the recent past? Yes.

The Victorian Football League (now Australian Football League) began, in effect, in 1897. Since then, some 11,000 players have participated in senior football, of whom only 115 have been Aborigines. Today, they star, soar, delight, infuriate, and win grand finals. Their ever- and omni-presence is hailed as normal. But between 1897 and 1980, there were only 20! It is ludicrous to argue that Aborigines didn't then have the speed, agility and musculature for this game, one they may well have invented. Several researchers suggest that *marn-grook*, an indigenous Victorian game played with a possum skin stuffed with pounded charcoal, was the basis for Australian football. It was characterised by the high leaping mark for the 'ball'.

The acceptance of the plethora of present players is belated and, until perhaps five years ago, grudging. The watershed was 1993. The notorious Collingwood fans gave St Kilda's Nicky Winmar a more-than-torrid dose of vilification. In response, he lifted his jumper and pointed proudly to his black skin. The press supported what in an earlier era would have been seen as 'cheeky nigger' behaviour. Collingwood president Allan McAlister told the television world that as long as 'they' behaved themselves like white folks off the field, they would be admired and respected; nay, it would be better, he said, if 'they' behaved themselves like human beings. By this time, the matter of racial vilification on the sports field had become a matter of public concern and serious media debate, resulting in the establishment of a meaningful code of conduct aimed at racial 'sledging'.

First division, however, is not the only division. Exclusion – being censored out – is rampant in the lower divisions, in country towns and remote communities. In Western Australia, South Australia and Victoria, several Aboriginal teams have been evicted from leagues, ostensibly on the grounds of bad spectator behaviour and worse language. Blue-rinse ladies in the Members' Stand at the Melbourne Cricket Ground shouting 'go sniff your petrol, you black fucking cunt' is *good* language?

So, too, with rugby league: dozens of black men do great things in senior football but, even as I write, there is exclusion of Aboriginal teams in three key New South Wales towns. This is disaster, indeed, because football in many of these hopeless, horizonless towns is often – as US writer HG Bissinger portrayed it so remarkably in *Friday Night Lights* – the sole purpose in life, the whole reason for being.

In both sports since the 1970s, Aborigines have sought all-Aboriginal teams. Outraged screams of 'apartheid' greet these calls. 'We're including you in,' say the officials in this 'land of the level playing field'; but the unstated reason is clear enough – without these black talents, they don't win premierships. Here, then, Aborigines are being censored in, rather than out. An all-Aboriginal rugby league side played two 'Tests' against Papua New Guinea last year – but officials are more than skittish about this 'trend'.

There is, regrettably, a more serious level of sports exclusion. Facilities in the majority of Aboriginal communities simply don't exist and words like oval, track, court, pool, gym, coach, physio, scholarship are not in the Aboriginal vocabulary or experience. If the costs of being able to participate in sport in rural and remote Australia are considered as a form of tax, then Aborigines pay higher taxes than any other group in Australia. Where access to organised competition is available, sponsorships are sparse and spare, with a few hundred dollars here and there for jerseys and boots. And Aboriginal women's sport is the most ignored, under-aided, under-funded activity in the Australian sporting world.

Until very recently, the Australian Sports Commission concerned itself solely with elite sport and with finding medal winners for international games. It has now come to recognise – very slowly and not quite convincedly – that sport for Aborigines is a matter of survival,

Rovers Football Club – Credit: Unknown

socially and physically, and that sport has a crucial role to play, not only in reducing delinquency but also in possible alleviation of Aboriginal youth suicide, now the highest rate on the planet. What no one wants to take on board is the correlation between sport and ill health – sport as panacea, sometimes treatment, or even cure for communities where coronary disease, respiratory disease, diabetes in particular, and deaths from non-natural causes (violence and accidents) are grossly prevalent.

Sport, leisure and recreation are singularly effective in treating diabetes and tuberculosis, and in 'diverting', or even thwarting, the at-riskness of high blood pressure, strokes and heart attacks. The twainness of sport and health, or lack of sport and ill health, is ignored.

For 40 years I have been lecturing about the Aboriginal experience, regaling students and readers with social indicators and vital statistics. Abstractions, really, until one shows the picture of the Rovers Football Club, winners in 1958 of an Australian football premiership in Ceduna, in South Australia's far west. When visiting in 1989, everyone urged me to meet Keith Willoughby (third from right at bottom). 'Why Keith?' I asked. 'Well, he's the only one alive', was the understated answer, 'and he can tell you all about winning the pennant'. A little investigation with Keith, who died in 1997, showed that 17 of the 18 lads didn't make it to age 50.

They died of most of the above-mentioned illnesses, including one suicide in custody. They died, in a sense, from life's exclusions, from isolation, contempt, denigration, from want of leisure or pleasure or place in society. Yes, they won a pennant – which also tells us that, while sport is significant in Aboriginal life, it is something that can't be played 365 days a year for indefinite years. Despite its limitations, it is the only arena in which Aborigines – unskilled, under educated, under fed, under-employed, unwell – can pit themselves against the mainstream, successfully, even if only for the briefest of moments. ❏

Colin Tatz is professor of politics at the University of Western Sydney. This year he has co-authored One-Eyed: A View of Australian Sport *and* Black Gold: the Aboriginal and Islander Sports Hall of Fame

MARGO KINGSTON

Crime and punishment

John Howard threatens to boycott international human rights committees in the interests of discriminating against Aborigines

In 1997, Australian Prime Minister John Howard ignored widespread legal opinion that his Native Title Amendment Bill 1997, which rolled back the land entitlements granted in the Mabo High Court judgement four years earlier, was racially discriminatory. He overrode protections offered by domestic racial legislation, leaving critics no alternative but to call in aid the international conventions on the topic.

Inevitably, the matter was taken to the UN, which made preliminary findings that the 'Wik law', as it is known, breached the Convention on the Elimination of all Forms of Racial Discrimination. For the first time in its history, Australia did not defend its actions by addressing the legal position; the government simply accused the committee of 'bias'.

Late last year, Howard himself invoked 'international human rights norms' to convince the UN to intervene in East Timor. The successful Australia-led mission prompted UN Secretary General Kofi Annan to visit Canberra in February to offer congratulations. Annan's arrival coincided with the explosion of another human rights issue that had been simmering for more than two years: Northern Territory laws giving judges no alternative but to send children to jail for petty theft:

> 'Receiving one bottle of spring water to the value of A$1.28 – 28 days; unlawfully entering a takeaway shop and stealing food and beverages to the value of A$18.50 – 14 days; stealing four slices of bread and cordial to the value of A$2.50 – 14 days.'

The effect of 'mandatory sentencing' – which included a 'white middle-class' exemption for shoplifting – was the jailing of a disproportionate number of Aboriginal children. After several adverse

UN reports, Howard assured the Northern Territory he would do nothing, despite his international obligations and a clear constitutional power to override the Territory's law-making apparatus.

The suicide early this year of a 15-year-old Aboriginal boy jailed for the theft of pens forced Howard to reconsider, and pressure mounted on Annan to raise the issue in his talks. Howard publicly urged Annan not to do so, saying Australia's human rights record was 'quite magnificent'. Annan complied. Howard claimed that Annan's silence in their February meeting meant the UN had given Australia a 'clean bill of health'.

Behind the scenes, the government was just as duplicitous. In March, Foreign Affairs Minister Alexander Downer released the UN's human rights report, which simply set out Australia's obligations under the conventions it has ratified. But, on 17 March, the *Sydney Morning Herald* reported that an intense diplomatic offensive had resulted in the UN report being scissored.

The original draft, altered after the government directly lobbied Annan to censor the report, said mandatory sentencing of children 'would appear to be in violation of international human rights standards prohibiting discrimination' and was 'a violation of the right to a fair trial by an independent and impartial court'. In another section expunged from the record, the authors affirmed: 'Mandatory sentencing rules are typically imposed by political authorities on the judiciary and they thus violate the usual requirement that the executive be separate and distinct from the judiciary.'

The issue reached its climax in Geneva in late March when the UN Committee on Racial Discrimination met to consider its finding on the Wik law, and to question Australia's representative, Phillip Ruddock, on mandatory sentencing. Again, intense diplomatic pressure was bought to bear. Again, the government produced no legal submission.

When the committee made adverse findings, the government did not stop at its usual claim that the UN was 'blatantly political and partisan'. In a surprise announcement on 30 March, the government said it had set up a top-level review of Australia's current participation in UN human rights committees, foreshadowing a possible boycott. At the time of writing, the review's findings were imminent. ❏

Margo Kingston is chief of staff in the Canberra bureau of the Sydney Morning Herald

Stolen generation

The 'Bringing them Home' inquiry heard the testimony of 535 Aboriginal and Torres Strait Islanders over the course of ten months from December 1995 to October 1996. Their testimonies describe the experiences of the 'stolen generation', who were forcibly fostered out to white families or church missions in order to 'assimilate' them into the white population. The legacy of this quiet genocide continues today

It was 1936. We had been playing all together, just a happy community, and the air was filled with screams because the police came and mothers tried to hide their children and blacken their children's faces and hide them in caves ... Six of us were put on an old truck and taken to Oodnadatta which was hundreds of miles away. From that time until 1968 I didn't see my mother. Thirty-two years it was.

> Fiona, confidential submission 305

I was taken away from [my mother]. Separating her from me was a grill. There was chicken wire across. I can remember sitting here at this grill on that side waiting for her to come out of the door of one of these wards there so that I can just see her. She wouldn't come out because it hurt her to see me over this side.

> Peggy, confidential evidence 404.

We had to learn to eat new food, have our heads shaved. We had to learn to sleep in a house. We'd only ever slept in our *wilchas* and always had the stars there and the embers of the fire and the closeness of the family. And all of a sudden we had high beds and that was very frightening. You just thought you were going to fall out.

> Fiona, confidential submission 305.

They told me that my family didn't care or want me and I had to forget them. They said it was degrading to belong to an Aboriginal family and

I should be ashamed of myself, I was inferior to whitefellas. They tried to make us act like white kids but, at the same time, we had to give up our seat for a whitefella because an Aboriginal never sits down when a white person is present.

  Millicent, confidential submission 640

They took us to a room and shaved our hair off ... They gave you your clothes and stamped a number on them ... They never called you by your name; they called you by your number. That number was stamped on everything. Every six months you were dressed up. Oh mate! You were done up beautiful – white shirt. The welfare used to come up from Bridge Street to check the home out – every six months.

  John, confidential submission 436.

If we answered an attendant back we were 'sent up the line'. Now I don't know if you can imagine 79 boys punching the hell out of you – just knuckling you. Even your brother, your cousin. They had to – if they didn't, they were sent up the line. Now that didn't happen once – that happened every day.

  John, confidential submission 436

We used to get whipped with a wet ironing cord and sometimes had to hold other children (naked) while they were whipped and, if we didn't hold them, we got another whipping. To wake us up in the morning we were sprayed up the backside with an old-fashioned pump fly-spray. Hurt was a part of our everyday life and we had to learn to live with it.

  Millicent, confidential submission 640.

I was sleeping in the caravan [at the foster parent's house]. I was only a little boy then. In the middle of the night somebody come to the caravan and raped me. That person raped me and raped me. I could feel the pain going through me. I cried and cried and they stuffed my head in the pillow. I had nobody to talk to. I don't know how long it went on for, but night after night I'd see the bogeyman.

  William, confidential submission 553.

From five and a half months old to 18 years of age, my mother never gave up trying to locate me. She wrote many letters to the State Welfare

Authorities pleading with them to give her son back. Birthday and Christmas cards were sent care of the Welfare Department. All these letters were shelved. The State Welfare Department treated my mother like dirt and with utter contempt, as if she never existed.

Paul, confidential submission 133.

Five generations of my family have been affected by the removal of children. Four generations of my family have been removed from their mothers and institutionalised. Four generations of my family went without parently love, without mother or father. I myself found it very hard to show any love to my children because I wasn't given that.

Carol, confidential submission 504

The Protector of Aborigines and the Child Welfare Department in their almighty wisdom said we would have a better life and future brought up as whitefellas away from our parents in a good religious environment. All they contributed to our upbringing and future was an unrepairable scar of loneliness, mistrust, hatred and bitterness. Fears that have been with me all of life. The empty dark and lonely existence was so full of many hurtful and unforgivable events that I cannot escape from, no matter how hard I try. Being deprived of the most cherished and valuable thing in life as an Aboriginal child – love and family bonds.

Millicent, confidential submission 640

I realised later how much I'd missed of my culture and how much I'd been devastated. Up until this point of time I can't communicate with my family, can't hold a conversation. Once that language was taken away, we lost a part of that very soul. It meant our culture was gone, our family was gone, everything that was dear to us was gone.

Fiona, confidential submission 305.

We were prisoners from when we were born. The girls who went to Cootamundra and the boys who went to Kinchela – we were all prisoners. Even today they have our file number, so we're still prisoners you know. And we'll always be prisoners while our files are in archives.

John, confidential submission 436 ❏

Compiled by **Melanie Clark**

PRIVACY

A *Social Research* Conference
New School University, New York City
Thursday, October 5 - Saturday, October 7, 2000

The Public/ Private Distinction	**The Household and Public Life** *Joseph Rykwert, U. Pennsylvania* **Reproductions of the Private** *Frederick Wiseman, Zipporah Films* **The Language of Privacy** *John Hollander, Yale* *Moderator: David Bromwich, Yale*
The Legal Construction of Privacy	**The History** *David Garrow, Emory* **Private Property** *David Richards, NYU* **The Internet and the Protection of Privacy** *Marc Rotenberg, EPIC* *Moderator: Frederick Schauer, Harvard*
Keynote Address	**Threats to Privacy** *Richard A. Posner, Chief Judge, Seventh Circuit*
Privacy and the Self: The Rise and Fall	**Sexuality, Shame and Intimacy** *Ruth Bernard Yeazell, Yale* **How Publicity Makes People Real** *David Bromwich, Yale* **Confessional Literature** *Nancy K. Miller, Graduate Center, CUNY* *Moderator: Louis Menand, Graduate Center, CUNY*
Invasions of Privacy: Violations of Boundaries	**Securing Privacy in an Electronic Age** *Lawrence Lessig, Stanford* **Privacy and Public Life** *Lewis H. Lapham, Harper's Magazine* **Privacy and the Freedom of Expression** *Frederick Schauer, Harvard* *Moderator: George Kateb, Princeton*
Privacy and the State	**Totalitarianism** *Fatos Lubonja, Perpjekja (Endeavor), Albania* **Privacy in a Decent Society** *Avishai Margalit, Hebrew U.* **Politics of Privacy** *George Kateb, Princeton* *Moderator: Jean Cohen, Columbia*
Is Privacy Possible? A Round Table Discussion	*Anita Allen Castellitto, U. Pennsylvania; Jean Cohen, Columbia; Esther Dyson, EDventure Holdings; Lewis H. Lapham, Harper's Magazine; Lawrence Lessig, Stanford; Theresa McGovern, Columbia; Philip Reitinger, Department of Justice; Maggie Scarf, Yale* *Moderator: Kenneth Prewitt, United States Census Bureau*

FOR INFORMATION AND TICKETS
Social Research Conferences
New School University, 65 Fifth Avenue, New York, NY 10003
Phone: (212) 229-2488 Fax: (212) 229-5476
E-mail: socres@newschool.edu
www.newschool.edu/centers/socres/privacy
Organized by Arien Mack, Editor

CHRIS MASTERS

Behind the wire

Twenty minutes from the Olympic stadium, a different kind of international village hides Australia's would-be asylum seekers

The first Australian sighted by increasing numbers of asylum seekers approaching these shores is a tall, suntanned seaman, pistol on hip, peering over the rail of a Royal Australian Navy patrol boat somewhere in the Timor Sea. People used to uniforms representing oppression say they are surprised when there is no rough treatment. The Australian military is tough but civilised. They conduct medical checks with sensitivity to individual custom. The galley has learned to cater for the Muslim diet.

The Australia-bound refugees, mostly from Iran and Afghanistan, have often marked time in a second country before risking a dangerous and expensive crossing from the southern tip of Indonesia. Their stories are the same as those from eastern Europe circa 1940, Cambodia in the 70s, and so on. 'The soldiers came in the night. They burned my home. My father was shot in front of me. I don't know what happened to my sister.'

They have heard Australia is a decent place, with an honourable human rights record. They are often fed nonsense by smugglers: that an amnesty is offered during the Olympic Games and there are plenty of jobs. The annual arrivals, now in their thousands, amount to a tiny proportion of the world's 20 million–plus displaced persons but they are sufficient to cause alarm. Unable to do much about the 'push' factors, Australia can address the 'pull' factors.It is not often a country sets out actively to downgrade its human rights record, but that appears to be what is happening.

The first big shock comes when the refugees arrive at the detention centre. Commonly it is Port Hedland, halfway up the West Coast. The 800-bed centre is surrounded by barbed wire, guards, desert scrub and

Child at Port Hedland – Credit: ABC

sea. There is little point in attempting escape. There is nowhere to run. The summer heat periodically kills stranded travellers. Port Hedland, Australia's only purpose-built immigration detention centre, is intentionally remote. It is more difficult to get out – and to look in.

The Department of Immigration and Multicultural Affairs (DIMA) does not generally allow media access. DIMA tells us the censorship is for the detainees' 'privacy and protection'. Identifying asylum seekers can harm home-country relatives. Applicants may also use the exposure unfairly to advance their case for asylum. If confined to conventional media deadlines, I could never have begun my television report, *A Well-Founded Fear of Persecution*. After months of negotiations, approval was given for me to take a camera to Port Hedland on an understanding that I screen out detainees' faces.

When I walked through the gate it was 42°C in the sun. People stuck to the shelter and the shadows. Guards accompanied us all the way. I knew I would not be shown the notorious Echo block where failed applicants await forced repatriation. There were a series of locked gates. DIMA isolates new arrivals to minimise the risk of coaching. Australia's Human Rights Commissioner Chris Sidoti complains it has trouble informing detainees of their rights.

I did see one of the classrooms: not a scene to forget. The teacher was strained and uncomfortable, using plastic fruit to introduce children to a new vocabulary: 'apple, pear, banana'. We were all uncomfortable. The question hung in the air. Why does Australia lock up innocent children? Some spend years behind the wire, while bureaucrats and lawyers debate their right to a protection visa and freedom.

Unlike comparable countries such as Canada, Australia stands by a policy of mandatory detention. People who have arrived without valid visas are locked up until their status is verified. Those who have questionable refugee credentials are detained for however long it takes – months or years. Those determined to be illegal immigrants are mostly swiftly removed.

The extra numbers have slowed the processing period. A new restriction, a three-year temporary visa, now makes the prospects of staying less certain. There are tragic scenes by the public telephone as detainees explain to wives and children in Pakistan and Iran that they may not be able to keep their promise of a new life in Australia.

Australia's policy of mandatory detention is condemned by Sidoti, who insists it is in breach of international law. Imprisonment is also regarded as a breach of United Nations High Commission for Refugees' guidelines. The government is untroubled by the criticism. Immigration detention is not much of a public issue. The Labor opposition sees little electoral mileage in trumpeting the cause of people commonly depicted in the media as illegals and queue jumpers. But the public doesn't know what goes on behind the wire.

We were not allowed into Villawood, the Sydney-based immigrant facility. We had to form a picture based on accounts of whistle-blower staff, escapees and the newly released. In doing so, we were introduced to the story of three Algerian detainees who had failed in their application for asylum and were awaiting removal. The men embarked on a hunger strike that brought them close to death. They were then flown from Sydney to a correctional centre in Brisbane. It is not uncommon for detainees to be arbitrarily removed to prisons.

The men were supposed to be force-fed. Attending doctor Stuart McDonald, appalled at what he saw, managed to persuade them to end their strike after obtaining a promise that their cases would be reviewed. It made no difference. Two of the men were removed from Australia in January – one on Australia Day. They were terrified, convinced that return to Algeria meant torture or death.

Both were later able to tell me about being bound and gagged and subjected to repeated forced injections of sedatives to quieten their protests on the aircraft. They spoke of being abused and humiliated. A shocked fellow passenger protested in the way many Australians might, if they too were allowed to bear witness. Amnesty International obtained a United Nations Committee Against Torture request to stay the removal of one of the men. It was ignored by the government. I was able to hear their stories because a bungle caused them to be offloaded in South Africa. One of the men, still distressed and terrified, recounted his experience. He said he had fled to Australia to escape such treatment.

The Villawood detention centre he left behind is only 20 minutes drive from the Olympic Stadium. Around 200 detainees make up an international village that can expect no showcasing come September. Villawood is a deeply unhappy place. The unhappiness will spread. The recent federal budget included an allocation for two new immigrant detention centres. ❏

Chris Masters is the senior reporter for the Australian Broadcasting Corporation's Four Corners *programme*

ROBBIE SWAN

Sex, life and video

How one man's vote drove sex off the agenda and into the black market

A ustralia has seen more censorship legislation pass through the federal parliament in the last few years than ever before in the country's history. The main reason was that a morals campaigner and representative of the conservative end of the Roman Catholic Church held the balance of power in the Senate at a time when a deeply conservative government needed his vote to pass two landmark pieces of legislation: a Goods and Services tax (GST) and to privatise Australia's lucrative, multimillion dollar telecommunications carrier, Telstra

Senator Brian Harradine, an ageing, independent politician from Tasmania who was returned by the barest of margins, made no secret that his main platform was anti-abortion, anti-pornography and anti-contraception. In return for his crucial vote on both the above, Harradine allegedly demanded the banning of live phone sex calls and a ban on adult sex sites on the Internet.

Phone sex services were effectively banned in late 1999 under the Telecommunications (Consumer Protection and Service Standards) Bill. The government used people's inherent sense of shame on sexual matters as the prime mover for the legislation. People who wanted the service were required to write a letter to the phone company outlining their innermost sexual preferences and thoughts before they could be connected. Calls to these services had been running at 1.5 million per month until the legislation was introduced: an audit of requests for the new 'opt-in' system (read 'ban') two months later, showed that only 30 people had written in. Senator and Minister of Telecommunications Richard Alston said that this showed that the majority of calls must have been placed by under-age boys.

On 1 January 2000, the Online Services Act came into force and created penalties of A$27,500 per day for Internet Service Providers (ISPs) who hosted otherwise legal X-rated (non-violent erotic) content or even R-rated content that had no means to stop access by children. The legislation was strongly opposed by almost every industry group, including the National Australia Bank and the ANZ Bank. It slowed down online traffic across the spectrum as ISPs were forced to employ costly devices to screen out rude words or images that contained more than 70% of flesh tone.

In September 1999, the federal government undertook a review of publications guidelines through the Office of Film and Literature Classification (OFLC). The guidelines now make it an offence to display 'breast nudity' on the cover of magazines in newsagents, notwithstanding the fact that most beaches attract large numbers of topless bathers. In the early 1970s, popular magazines featured full nudity on their covers without legislative censure. Conservative politicians also succeeded in lobbying the OFLC to initially ban the French art-house film *Romance*. After a very public debate, the decision was overturned by the Classification Review Board.

However, a bill introduced last year to raise a tax on all film, video, publication and computer games – under the guise of a 'classification fee' – was defeated in the Senate when the opposition parties grouped together to vote it down. The Classification Charges Bill would have set the first tax in Australia that did not have to go back to parliament to be changed. This could have been done by public servants in the form of a regulation, and would have set the scene for a regime of 'economic' censorship. Sexually oriented and other 'controversial' books and films would have been made subject to additional taxes because they did not meet with the moral codes of certain bureaucrats. Though the government gave the entertainment industry assurances that this would not have happened, the Eros Foundation combined with the mainstream Australian Independent Distributors Association to lobby the opposition against the legislation. Interestingly, the large Hollywood distributors in Australia gave tacit support to the tax, possibly seeing it as an opportunity to knock out small and independent film-makers.

Australia's television guidelines were also changed to meet Senator Harradine's wishes. He had long fought to ban the Ten Network's high-rating *Sex/Life* programme. When the show went into recess, he managed to persuade Senator Alston, the minister for telecommunications, to twist the arm of the self-regulatory television body, FACTS, to ensure that the level of sexual depiction in *Sex/Life* could not be shown. Again, the level of sexual information screened in the 1970s, via soaps and sitcoms like *Number 96* and *The Box*, was far higher, and *Sex/Life* has attracted few complaints from the public.

All adult computer games are also banned. The previous Labor government implemented the ban and the present coalition government increased its reach. It did this by asking the OFLC to regard a computer game as one level higher than the 'level of depiction' would normally have received as a film or video, claiming that the interactive nature of a computer game made it more 'potent'. The argument was never substantiated by research.

The last few years have seen our sex industry lobby group, Eros Foundation, become increasingly active in opposing censorship. A series of nationwide opinion polls has shown that most adults support explicit sexual depictions of non-violent erotica, but are less happy with violent or racist depictions. Eros commissioned Roy Morgan Research (the company that polls for both major political parties) to undertake most of the surveys.

Eros president Fiona Patten said: 'The government's attempts to "bribe" Senator Harradine into voting for the GST by offering him bans on phone sex lines, adult Internet sites, sexually oriented television programmes and a million-dollar boost to Tasmania's economy were greeted very cynically by the general public, and fostered the view that official censorship policies could be easily corrupted for short-term political gain.'

One of the most remarkable figures from the poll was that 73% of respondents supported the availability of non-violent erotic videos from licensed adult shops. When Eros polled on the issue in 1996 using the AGB McNair group, it got a 72% support for this same question and, in 1992, it was 70% support. Politicians need to be wary of outlawing the product. When they do, they become responsible for setting up the black market that inevitably results. ❏

Robbie Swan is campaign manager and publisher at Eros Foundation, an alliance of sex industry companies fighting for more rational legislation on morals

JANE MILLS

Two smacks & out!

A crackdown on sex in film and TV reverses Australians' one-time right to 'see, read and listen to whatever they choose'

When the future of reconciliation between indigenous Australians and those of white settler stock is at risk because Prime Minister John Howard has banned the word 'sorry' from his vocabulary, it might seem trivial to worry about film censorship. All that's apparently happening is an attempt to ban the representation of an erect penis here, a blow job there and a spot of S&M wherever. But in recent years, with absolutely no evidence of significant public demand, the freedom of every 'reasonable adult' to 'read, see, or hear whatever they choose' – a right supposedly enshrined in federal legislation – has been restricted by insidious censorship creep.

In 1995, the Spanish anti-neo-Nazi film *Tras el cristal* was banned from a film festival – an event previously considered immune from censorship. The following year, the various state censorship ministers approved more restrictive classification guidelines for films and videos. In 1997, the federal government came close to banning sexually explicit, non-violent videos. Now that it was possible for previous classification decisions to be reviewed, Pasolini's polemic against fascism, *Salo*, having been unbanned in the early 1990s after 17 years of prohibition, was once again banned. Meir Zarchi's rape-revenge movie, *I Spit on Your Grave* (once voted Australia's top horror movie), suffered a similar fate.

The scene was set for collaboration between the fiercely censorious Senator Brian Harradine and the minority Liberal government. Declaring inexperience to be more valuable than expertise, the latter set up a series of 'community groups' to monitor the decisions of the Office of Film and Literature Classification. The official classifiers were 'reassessed' and new ones appointed largely on the basis of a stated preference for parents, especially mothers.

Rocco Siffredi in Romance – *Credit: Tana Kayela/SIPA*

Very few of those now responsible for deciding what a notional 'reasonable adult' may see in the cinema possess much, if any, understanding of the basics of a screen education. Understanding an art form that relies upon a distinction between fantasy and actuality, by using realism to represent the illusion of reality, is beyond our classifiers and censoring ministers who would definitely fail to secure a pass grade in Film Studies 101. The post-modern, queer film *Hustler White*, for example, was refused classification because of its representation of

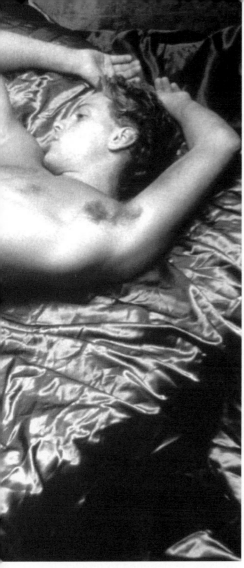

consenting sex in the form of some realistic masturbation and some very unrealistic buttock-slashing. Jim Jarmusch's acclaimed film *Dead Man* was initially refused classification because of four seconds depiction of non-consenting fellatio.

Early this year the same thing happened to Catherine Breillat's art-house movie *Romance*, featuring Rocco Siffredi's magnificent erectile tissue. Initially, the realistic consenting sex in this film was deemed unacceptable for cinema audiences, but acceptable for consumers of video pornography. The clearly dramatised, non-consenting sex (a rape depicting the heroine as survivor rather than victim), however, was considered unacceptable for video pornography, but acceptable for cinema audiences. The decision was overturned after protests from screen critics, film-makers, broadcasters and others in the industry – precisely the sort of experts no longer valued as classifiers.

Absurdity is the name of the game. We can watch a sexy spanking on prime-time television in *Ally McBeal*, but we can't watch a rerun of the 1970s popular soap *Number 96*, which featured a naked woman – and a former deputy chief censor, who transmogrifies into the producer of porn videos with titles such as *Buffy Down Under*.

It gets more bizarre. The price Senator Harradine exacted for his support took the form of a government bill on 'Non-Violent Erotica', banning depictions of anything other than very mild fetishism – one

JANE MILLS

smacked bottom, yes: two smacks, no. Outlawed would be representations of perfectly legal activities – body piercing, candle wax applications, golden showers, defecation, bondage, spanking and fisting. At the eleventh hour, however, Harradine led a successful rout and opposed the bill originally made to his own specifications, demanding the name of the bill be changed from 'pornography' to 'erotica'. The attorney-general was left with egg on his chin when no one, not even his prime minister and the responsible arts minister (both of whom joined Harradine in the lobby) bothered to inform him of this about-turn.

This particular circus promises to turn into something more bloody, with the porn industry (which supports the concept of non-violent erotica) threatening to 'out' all those – politicians and their voters – who buy their X-rated material. The pusillanimous Labor opposition, meanwhile, supports the pornographers but refuses to argue against the explicit censorship of the bill. There are no votes in screen spanking.

The silliness of events conceals something more ominous. The Howard government has deflected what should be a debate about human rights and freedoms into one of obligations, turning the issue of free speech into one of national identity. The freedom of citizens to see films that encourage sexual or political diversity is promoted as being somehow 'un-Australian'. A 'true blue' Aussie, or so the argument goes, has an obligation to rid the screen of anything other than straight vanilla sex – and traditional conservative politics. Can it be an accident that most of the films banned, censored or cut recently are those valued by political and sexual libertarians, as well as many gays and feminists?

It is as hypocritical for legislators to persist in the claim that all adult Australians may 'see, read and listen to whatever they choose', as it is for politicians to pretend our classification laws are designed to protect community values by safeguarding the sensibilities of the 'reasonable adult'. There is plenty of evidence to suggest that our politicians believe their voters to be neither reasonable nor mature. ❏

Jane Mills is head of screen studies at the Australian Film, Television and Radio School and a founding member of Australia's Watch On Censorship committee

152   INDEX ON CENSORSHIP 4 2000

IRENE GRAHAM

Purity postponed

In April 1999 the Australian government's proposed Internet legislation sent shockwaves around the world, prompting an outcry from anti-censorship activists. In June 2000, six months after the law commenced, Australian Internet users have noticed little difference, but the long-term threat to free expression remains

From 1995 to 1997 the government conducted four inquiries into censoring the Internet and a draft legislative framework was issued in mid-1997. However, it was not until two years later that significantly harsher legislation was rushed through parliament. Many concluded the motivation was something other than 'widespread community concern'.

The October 1998 election had hit the government's prospects of passing several key pieces of legislation. Until 1 July 1999, the balance of power in the Senate would remain with an independent, Brian Harradine, one of Australia's most vocal censorship apostles. The legislation was therefore widely perceived to be an attempt to obtain Harradine's vote for other controversial bills (see p146).

The new scheme is 'complaints based' and applies to material on Web and ftp (file transfer protocol) sites, and in newsgroups, but does not include content in Internet relay chat and email. It comprises a complex mass of regulation involving the Australian Broadcasting Authority (ABA), the Office of Film and Literature Classification (OFLC), a new government-appointed board named NetAlert, Commonwealth legislation and a raft of proposed State enforcement legislation.

Material becomes 'prohibited content' only if it is complained about and then classified by the ABA or the OFLC using criteria originally developed for films and videos. As this criteria was developed for moving images and sound, Internet content consisting largely of text and static images is now subject to more restrictive censorship than equivalent material in offline publications.

Prohibited content is that classified Refused Classification (RC), which is material that 'offends against the standards of morality, decency and propriety generally accepted by reasonable adults', or classified X (non-violent sexually explicit material involving adults only). Material classified R (unsuitable for persons under 18 years) is also prohibited if it is hosted in Australia and access is not restricted by an ABA-approved adult verification system – access is blocked unless a purchased password or credit-card details are entered.

In the case of Australian-hosted content, if the ABA decides it is likely to be classified X or RC, the procedure is to issue an interim takedown notice. Once classified by the OFLC, the ABA either issues a final takedown notice or revokes the interim notice. Final takedown notices are also issued for R-classified content that is not held behind an adult verification system. Hosts must remove content by 6pm on the next working day or face fines of up to AU$27,500 (US$16,450) per day.

Since foreign sites cannot be forced to comply, the government initially envisaged requiring Internet Service Providers (ISPs) to block access to overseas content classified X or RC. However, after industry advice that this was not possible, the legislation was amended to require blocking if 'technically and commercially feasible'.

As to further regulation, the legislation offers industry two choices: develop a Code of Practice compliant with the Act, or else face a mandatory 'Industry Standard'. Several months after the legislation was passed in June 1999, Senator Richard Alston, the minister for communications, continued to insist that parental/user empowerment was not sufficient in the government's view and that ISPs must block sites. Nevertheless, a Code of Practice that does not require blocking was prepared by the Internet Industry Association of Australia (IIA) and approved by the ABA in December. However, the ABA will review the Code shortly and, as noted above, can develop and mandate an Industry Standard if the Code of Practice is found to be deficient.

As it stands, the IIA Code requires ISPs to 'provide' an Approved Filter to each of their customers, unless the particular customer 'has advised their ISP that he or she already has installed an Approved Filter'. The Code permits ISPs to choose whether to 'provide' a server-side filter (installed on the ISPs' computers) or a client-side filter (installed on the user's machine). However, users do not *have* to use any filter provided and, in any event, many ISPs simply offer filters if asked. Also, instead of the ABA notifying ISPs to block content as the government originally intended, the ABA now notifies Approved Filter suppliers of content they consider is likely to be classified X or RC.

So what has been the effect of this complex regime? By 31 March 2000 the ABA had received just 124 complaints and investigated 99. Except for two involving newsgroup articles, all investigations involved Web content. Sixty-six items of prohibited content were identified; 35 hosted outside Australia and 31 in Australia. Once notified of complaints, 17 of 23 items hosted in Australia moved to overseas servers. In all, as a result of 99 investigations, just 11 items were actually removed from the Internet and 52 were notified to the makers of Approved Filters.

It is doubtful that the scheme has hit freedom of expression in Australia and, in any case, the option of using an overseas host remains. Australians are still free to see what they wish on the Internet, or to choose to use a filter for their family's Internet access; an option available to them long before the government got involved.

But the future is anyone's guess. The government or the ABA may well decide the ISP Code is deficient; State and Territory governments may enact laws involving prior restraint on Internet users' speech; complaints may increase, forcing more sites offshore.

On the other hand, a current or future government may acknowledge that the law does not and cannot protect children, and that the millions of dollars allocated to enforcing it would be better spent on the education programme promised by all governments in recent years.

The most alarming aspect of the regime is that it may give parents a false sense of security where their children's use of the Internet is concerned, since the government loudly implies it has solved the problem. Protecting children on the Internet requires adults in Australia, as elsewhere, to supervise those in their care, as it always will, irrespective of the Australian government's attempt to 'do something'. ❑

Irene Graham is executive director of Electronic Frontiers Australia (EFA). More at www.efa.org.au

CHRISTINE NICHOLLS

Cutting edge

The end of bilingual education in English and Aboriginal languages is threatened along with reconciliation and co-operation between the races, along with any prospect of raising educational standards among Aborigines

In December 1998, the Northern Territory (NT) government decided to disband its unique bilingual education programmes in which local Aboriginal languages and English were used in primary-school classrooms, and replace them exclusively with instruction in English. At that time in NT schools, there were 21 bilingual education programmes in which 17 different indigenous languages were being taught.

It is difficult to interpret the NT's decision – endorsed by the federal education minister – as anything but a direct attack on the few remaining 'strong' Aboriginal languages. The decision also means the 'demobilisation' of many dedicated bilingual education workers in remote rural communities, the majority of them Aboriginal. This will translate into higher rates of unemployment among rural Australians.

Bilingual education has been under almost constant attack since its introduction by the Federal Labor government of Gough Whitlam in 1973 as part of a set of reforms under the general imprimatur of self-determination for indigenous Australians and because of the total failure of English-only programmes in Aboriginal schools.

For almost a decade, I lived and worked with the Warlpiri at Lajamanu, a settlement roughly equidistant from Alice Springs and Darwin in the Tanami Desert. We worked to establish a successful bilingual education programme using Warlpiri and English. Under the leadership of two visionaries, the late Maurice Luther Jupurrurla and the late Paddy Patrick Jangala, the Lajamanu community had lobbied government for ten years before the school was officially recognised.

Protest postcard featuring Yolngu Matha people, NT, Australia

Older people feared that young Warlpiri were in danger of losing their culture and language. Older Warlpiri recollect English being imposed upon them by pure force. A Warlpiri friend, Peggy Rockman Napurrurla, recalls those days of linguistic suppression: 'In the Welfare Days the settlement supervisors would hit us if we spoke Warlpiri. They would say: "Stop talking in that Chinese language."'

So committed was the community that, in 1982, ten Warlpiri adults worked full-time for the entire year with no pay to create Warlpiri books for Warlpiri children to read. The success of the programme could be measured in both academic and social terms. In 1989, the school topped all government Aboriginal schools in the NT in the education department's externally-administered testing programmes in English.

Aboriginal-controlled bilingual programmes give parents and extended families a real place in their children's education. Bilingual education put Aboriginal teachers into classrooms as 'real' teachers, thereby acting as circuit-breakers to continuing welfare dependence. Their presence improved relations between the community members and schools, increasing school attendance, strengthening minority languages and raising the self-esteem of both adults and children. Early learning in one's first language enables children to acquire a second

CHRISTINE NICHOLLS

language with greater ease. English as a second language and bilingual education are mutually supportive. As Mandawuy Yunupingu, lead singer of the band Yothu Yindi and a former principal of Yirrkala Bilingual School, put it: 'If you have control over both languages, you have double power'.

The decision to scrap the bilingual education programmes represents a return to the White Australia days. This long predates the government's 1950s Frankenstein-type dream of assimilation for indigenous Australians as well as migrants. As early as 1838, the governor of South Australia made a speech to the Kaurna Aboriginal people of the Adelaide Plains in which he exhorted 'the natives' to drop their languages in favour of English: 'Blackman, we wish to make you happy. But you can not be happy unless you imitate white man. Build huts, wear clothes and be useful ... have God ... love white men ... and learn to speak ENGLISH' (original emphasis).

Tragically, the last fluent speaker of Kaurna died in 1929. Indeed, three-quarters of Australia's 250 indigenous languages have already been extinguished by colonisation, a loss not only for Australia but for the world's linguistic heritage. These languages are living treasures, and it is clear from the outrage being expressed in parts of remote Aboriginal Australia (communities are threatening to pull their children out when the next school year begins) that the NT's decision isn't 'making them happy'. So strong is the reaction that, over the past 18 months, Aboriginal communities have campaigned under the catchcry 'Don't Cut Off Our Tongues'. In late 1999, the largest petition in NT history was presented to the NT parliament, protesting at cuts which were made without consulting any Aboriginal community.

The philosophy and practice of bilingual education provided a virtually unparalleled opportunity for genuine indigenous and non-indigenous reconciliation, requiring, as it does, co-operation, team-teaching and other interactions based on sharing knowledge and space. But it appears that, in terms of the linguistic genocide that has been prosecuted in this country, the NT, in collusion with the Howard government, is now presiding over the 'final solution'. ❑

Christine Nicholls is the head of cultural studies and senior lecturer in Australian studies at the Flinders University of South Australia. From 1982 to 1991, she was principal of Lajamanu School in the Tanami Desert

Culture

Two articles look at the relationship between cricket and society. In England, imperial decline is mirrored on 22 yards of green. In the West Indies, the long struggle for a place on the pitch parallels battles for political autonomy.

Plus: Aborigine poetry.

DIRAN ADEBAYO

Batting collapse

Kensington Oval, Port of Spain, Trinidad, February 1994. West Indies v England. After lasting maybe 20 minutes in the prime seats largely occupied by those, like us, who've come from Britain we – my two white friends and I – have decamped to a locals' stand. Here, the Nutsman, his natties packed under a striped top hat and over his shoulder a body-long canvas bag, stuffed with every known nut in the world, is moving among us, slinging his wares around, and pitching with ditties in his Trini lilt: 'Nuts, Nuts! How many? Is it any?' ... 'You grow big on nuts and honey/All that's missing is your money ...' 'Nuts! Special Lara nuts, special Lara rates...'

Each over's end is punctuated by blasts of soca and reggae from the many sound systems in the ground, and the sight of an old, cross-dressed man, a much-loved 'Mistress of Misrule', gyrating his double-jointed triple-skirted self. All of the island's worlds seem represented across the packed ground, from the middle classes to young ragamuffins, from those who have no especial love for the game but are patriots still, to the connoisseurs, hunched silently over their scorecards, or else swapping judgements like lords of the earth.

There is rum and beer and any amount of addictive dice-and-counters games to be played during the breaks. My England-supporting spars exchange much banter with our new friends and, as paceman Curtly Ambrose's wickets help to scuttle England for 46, the nuts are magically transformed to 'Ambrose nuts'. On the final day, an excited buzz goes round as three of the island's most celebrated calypsonians appear below us, guitars in hand, ready to serenade the expected home victory. And as we join the hundreds behind them surging to the pavilion, all three of us are beaming, so happy to have seen what we've seen, to have sampled our favourite thing in such an environment.

'Boy!' one of my friends turned to me, mindful of all the talk there had been about the decline in interest in cricket in the Caribbean, 'it would be nice to have a decline like this back home!'

Back home, of course, music was banned. Faced with increasingly vocal supporters of Pakistan and the West Indies, who blew horns, whistles and banged drums at their teams' triumphs, the English cricketing authorities had responded by banning these instruments from its grounds, treating its latest chance to broaden its appeal with the scorn and the blinkered vision I had come to expect.

If Britain's post-war history is a story of the management of the decline of a once world power, then there is no more dramatic case study than that of English cricket. Attendances at the first-class game have slumped from 2.3 million in 1946 to a tenth of that now, while the briefest stroll through this country's streets and parks will tell you of the almost complete eviction of the game from the social fabric. In times that have been increasingly populist-minded any activity that reeked of the old class dispensations was always going to struggle. English cricket needed to reinvent and re-align itself, but it didn't.

A part of me – the hanging judge in me – feels quite unmoved by this situation. English cricket has been hoisted on its reactionary petard; the fitting historical end point to a 200-year process – most recently and most brilliantly documented in Mike Marqusee's *Anyone But England: Cricket and the National Malaise* – in which cricket is less of a game, and more about the dissemination of an establishment ethic, to be spread through the nation's classes and its imperial possessions. But the greater part of me remains stunned and so saddened, especially when that first gorgeously distinctive tang of summer grass comes through in May, to see a game that was still all around in the streets and parks of inner-city London when my brothers and I were growing up in the 1970s, so reduced. And, though it's a pleasure to fly in the face of this rather conformist age, and all the point-seeking phonies that have jumped on football's dick, it's a pleasure I do not share often, lest someone, ignorant of my approach to the game, mistake me for old Britain.

Cricket had come easily to me, the way it could to children, writers, and other con-connoisseurs. Like most kids I loved play, and mischief, and mischief in my play most of all. Tricks, things not being what they seemed ... these were pleasures I would soon be discovering in books, but marginally before the Word there was sport, whose glorious principle seemed to me to be beating people with tricks. And so, in football I loved to dribble, in rugby, when it came, I loved to sidestep and dummy, and in cricket I loved to spin the ball. With all the multiple variations that could be produced with the merest, imperceptible adjustments to your finger action, spinning, as we all know now in these New Labour times, is dissemblers' heaven.

There were other elemental qualities in the game too. Batting I found to be the most resonant, deeply terrifying of experiences. Unlike, say, football, where individual battles were swiftly buried under group exertions and where the faulty were given opportunities to find redemption, in cricket the spotlight was always shining on the duel between bat and ball, and the batsman had no untold chances to hide behind. I would stand there, insides a flutter, as the bowler ran towards me, knowing that if I made a single mistake, I would be 'out'. Finished. Dead. Here, every moment, a man was in danger of meeting his fate.

In short, where others saw a good old team game, I saw gladiatorial combat; long before I heard that cricket was about honour and decency, I thought it was about lies. I was not, sport was quickly to teach me, a very 'English' boy. I was the one who'd be out there on the right wing, trying my occasional flashy-moves trickery, only to be substituted by the exasperated football coach and replaced by some drone with a harder working ethic. Or the one who, affecting a slouch on the cricket field, hoping to tempt the opposition batsman into a rash run, would be subjected to constant shells from the little Hitler leading us, outraged at my 'improper demeanour' and be dropped down the bowling list.

Needless to say, I stopped playing the game within such official structures just as soon as I possibly could, only to find that that same high-English curse of propriety was increasingly affecting my consumption of the game, witness the hoo-hah over music at grounds.

The tragic, little-known fact is that English cricket was not always like this. There was a time, in the early part of the nineteenth century, before it became institutionalised, before the public schools got to grips with it, when the game was more in touch with its and people's basic pleasures. As Marqusee recalls: 'An air of festive exhibition hung about all the great matches. Single-wicket contests ... handicapping of various kinds gave cricket a circus-like ambience. People came to see the great champions. It was a jocular, picaresque pastime, an occasion to eat and drink.'

In my novel, I bring the flavours of this old England and the present-day Caribbean to my account of a cricket match set in a near-future London. The government's Minister for Special Duties, a sort of Minister for PR figure, has set up 'Sports Day', an annual public holiday on which a one-day grudge cricket match is played between the poor Rest and the rich West of the city, in the hope that a high-profile encounter of the civilising gentlemen's game will dissipate social tensions. The Nutsmen are in there, there are gaming stalls and sound systems in there, for those who want to hear them, and the crowds most definitely are in there. It is cricket as gladiatorial spectacle, cricket as a space that can include the unconverted, cricket understood as an accompaniment to, not a suspension of everyday pleasures. Cricket as an arena to reflect, not, say, redundant old counties, but more contemporary affiliations, cricket as a game where supporters are being 'British' in different ways.

A somewhat nightmarish social scenario but not, perhaps, such a bad prescription for a, ahem, rebranding of 'the national summer game', particularly at a time when football is ever more money-minded, less, in a certain sense, of the people. Just a thought. Whatever the precise ingredients, if English cricket is to pull itself out of the margins, then it needs a little bit of its old, a little bit of the not so foreign, and it needs to harness them fast. ❏

Diran Adebayo is the author of the novels My Once Upon A Time *and* Some Kind of Black, *both published by Abacus.*

CLR JAMES

Cricket in West Indian culture

From its beginning to this day cricket in the West Indies has expressed with astonishing fidelity the social relations of the islands. The early island teams consisted for the most part of the Englishmen in the colonies associated with local whites, and black plebeians who were dignified by the title of professional bowlers. These bowlers were more ground attendants than professionals in the accepted modern sense. Some of them had come to the nets where their betters practised, picked up the ball and bowled, sometimes without shoes.

The brown-skin or black middle class produced a few good players but there was a sharp social gap between Englishmen and white or light-skinned members of the upper classes and the black plebeians who bowled so well that they were sometimes given an opportunity to make a precarious living by their skill. The black population of those days seemed to accept the conditions. They welcomed the Englishmen uproariously and even seemed to support them more than the local side.

Between 1900 and 1939 the development of West Indian society improved the status and conditions of the coloured middle classes with effective results in the organisation of cricket as a national expression. In addition to clubs exclusively white, with perhaps a few coloured men of wealth or distinction, the brown-skinned middle class also formed their own clubs. So did the black-skinned middle class. In time the black plebeians also formed their own. These divisions (not always in every island iron-clad) were not only understood but accepted by players and populations alike. All these clubs played every Saturday in club competitions and not infrequently a white member of the Legislative Council or president of the Chamber of Commerce would be playing amicably for his club against another, most of whose members were

black porters, messengers or other members of the lowest social classes. Cricket was therefore a means of national consolidation. In a society very conscious of class and social differentiation, a heritage of slavery, it provided a common meeting ground of all classes without coercion or exhortation from above.

English expatriates and their local associates retained their dominance in cricket not merely by social prestige and money but by their services. The wealthier clubs of the upper classes usually assumed the responsibility of inviting MCC teams and arranged for West Indian teams to visit England in 1900 and 1906. The black professional players were included and by 1928 the West Indies were granted Test matches. The outstanding personality in their steady advancement of the game was a Barbados white man – HGB Austin, a fine player and very successful business-man whose father had been bishop of the West Indies.

Yet the expatriate Englishmen and the local white aristocracy, with some few coloured men who had won acceptance in these circles, were not the decisive forces in the inculcation of the cricket ethic which has so shaped and permeated West Indian social life. This was done by English university men, chiefly from Oxford and Cambridge. During the last third of the 19th and the first third of the 20th centuries many of these were masters at the secondary schools in the larger territories and their social influence went far beyond their actual numbers.

At these schools for many years there were some 200 boys, children of Englishmen and local whites, many sons of the brown-skinned middle class, Chinese, Indians, and black boys, often poor who had won some of the very few scholarships to these schools, and others, not too many, whose parents could afford it. These Oxford and Cambridge men taught us Latin and Greek, mathematics and English literature, but they also taught, rather diffused, what I can only call the British public-school code.

The success of this code inside the classrooms was uncertain. On the playing fields, especially the cricket field, it triumphed. Very rapidly we learned to 'play with the team', which meant subordinating your personal inclinations and even interests to the good of the whole. We kept a 'stiff upper lip' in that we did not complain about ill fortune. We did not denounce failure but 'well tried' or 'hard luck' came easily to our lips. We were generous to opponents and congratulated them on victories, even when we knew they did not deserve them. We absorbed the same discipline through innumerable boys' books: books by GA Henty, the 'Mike' stories by PG Wodehouse, school magazines like *The Captain*. Generation after generation of boys of the middle class went through this training and experience, and took it out into the West Indian world with them, the world of the games they continued to play and the world outside. The masses of the people paid little attention to this code but they knew it, and one condition of rising to a higher status in life was obedience or at least obeisance to it.

To the degree that cricket embodied a national consolidation so much needed by the islands, it could not fail to express the growing consciousness of social differentiation. Though for a long time in the West Indies the value of the services and the authority in cricket of men like HBG Austin was unquestioned, cricket was a field where the social passions of the colonials, suppressed politically, found vigorous if diluted expression. On the cricket field all men, whatever their colour or status, were theoretically equal. Clubs of the lower-middle class or black men who achieved international status were passionately supported by the mass of the population, and in return this section seemed to play with an energy and fire which indicated that they were moved by the sense of being representative which circumstances had thrust upon them. Members of various classes gave a moral support to teams and players of their own class, though my personal experience is that this sharp racial competitiveness very rarely caused any departure from the high principles of cricket sportsmanship, and sharpened the game.

Individual players of the lower class, most often black men, became popular national heroes in whom the masses of the people took great pride. Yet it is doubtful if any player was more nationally admired and more of a popular idol than the late George Challenor, a white Barbadian and a member of the most exclusive of white Barbados clubs.

In one particular respect the growth of nationalist sentiment has invaded the cricket field and coloured public response to it. From the beginning the captaincy of the separate island teams was looked upon as an almost impenetrable preserve of the local whites. After WWII, however, public opinion and the number of fine players emerging from the middle classes and the plebeians made this preserve difficult to maintain and before long it broke down. But the captaincy of the West Indies team remained the patent source of social division. The explosions during the MCC tours in 1953 and 1960 were not in any way directed against British players or as representatives of the imperial power. In fact, although the 1960 explosion in Trinidad, when the crowd threw bottles on the field and brought a day's play in a Test match to a premature close, took place at the height of a great agitation for national independence, no anti-British sentiments were either felt or manifested and the British players were very popular. The social antagonisms which the outburst undoubtedly expressed were completely internal. They were directed against what was widely considered to be the persistent manipulation by the traditional authorities aimed at maintaining the privileges which, natural in the earlier days, were now held to be out of place. It was widely felt that for years conscious and indefensible efforts had been made to maintain the exclusion from the West Indies captaincy of men black in skin. It needed a vigorous campaign and a massive exhibition of popular feeling before Frank Worrell, a black man, was appointed captain of the West Indies team to Australia. Now organised cricket and soccer are both democratic and popular national institutions in the West Indian territories, which badly need such institutions.

More important still, Frank Worrell has shown that a black man can be an exceptional leader. One incident on the 1957 tour illustrates this well.

One of the black fast bowlers was Gilchrist, whose career is a perfect symbol of the stresses and strains of West Indian social and political life. The twenty-first child of a rural family of twenty-one children, he was brought from the rural districts of Jamaica by a local businessman, given a job and forthwith showed his unusual energies and ability for big cricket. He went to India with the West Indies team, but had to be sent home for conduct unsatisfactory to the West Indian management. In Trinidad in 1960 posters appeared asking the public to boycott the game unless Gilchrist was selected. Regardless of the charges made or charges proved, a great mass of the population feels that Gilchrist represents them and any action taken against him is an action against them, and he has become known as a stormy petrel of the game. Yet I witnessed a most revealing incident at Hastings in 1957. Gilchrist, a member of the touring team, was told by his captain that in festival cricket one did not bowl bumpers. Determined to oblige, Gilchrist allowed himself to be driven for five fours in one over: a notably tempestuous member or a tempestuous breed, fast bowlers, Gilchrist was determined not to offend his captain for that day – a middle-class black West Indian, Frank Worrell. He alone seemed able to exercise influence over the ebullient plebeian.

In one of his novels George Lamming, the Barbados novelist, has declared in the most unequivocal terms that the educated black middle classes must accept responsibility for whatever attitude to accepted standards may be shown by the black masses: 'Nor can I allow my own moral infirmity to be transferred to a foreign conscience, labelled imperialist.' The relationship between Worrell, the Jamaican senator with an economics degree from Manchester, and the plebeian Gilchrist indicates the tensions demanding resolution in the developing future of the islands, but also what cricket can do to restore them.

The West Indian's very consciousness of his own history is a product of his cricket in a very definite sense. In Britain, Drake and mighty Nelson, Shakespeare, the Charge of the Light Brigade, the success of parliamentary democracy, the few who did so much for so many – these constitute a continuous national tradition. Underdeveloped, newly independent countries have to go back many decades, sometimes centuries, to find one. The West Indian people have none, at least none that they know anything about. To such people, Ramadhin and Valentine wrecking English batting, the three Barbados batsmen whose names begin with W, the front-page scoring of cricketers like Garfield Sobers and Rohan Kanhai fill gnawing gaps in their consciousness and in their needs. Hence the popular passions which have on occasion overstepped the bounds. Yet when over a quarter of a million people in an Australian city came into the streets to tell Worrell's team goodbye, a spontaneous gesture of affection and respect, the West Indies, clearing their way with bat and ball, had made a public entry into the comity of nations. It has been done under the aegis of the men who more than all others created the British public-school tradition, Thomas Arnold, Thomas Hughes and WG Grace. They would recognise Frank Worrell as a representative of all they were and stood for. But juniors grow up and have to make their own independent way. In cricket, the West Indies have evolved a style of their own, even if in independence as a whole they have yet to do so. ❏

CLR James (1901-1989) was a cultural historian and a leading figure in the Pan-African movement. His books include The Black Jacobins *(1938) and* Beyond a Boundary *(1963).*
This article was first published in New Society, *6 June 1963, collected in the anthology* Cricket, *Allison & Busby, 1986*

ROMAINE MORETON

The Silence of Blackness

The silence of blackness,
that struggles for voice,
    within these walled institutions
    and
    out,
where my voice contradicts your silence,
    as yours does mine,
where legislated thought does not always consider me,
but I must never disregard the paper
    upon which it is written,

My spirit is forced to wade
    through channels of technological sewerage
    and hegemonic refuse,

And while my thoughts travel different cultural roads,
    having to overcome obstacles and blockades
    put in place by the black thought police,

Yours are allowed to travel upon great constructions
of permanence,
    Freeways of mind with little hindrance,

My vehicle is my body that houses my soul,

    and you,

the technology that attempts to determine its route,

My blackness is more than thought,
>   it is speech,
>   it is seeing,
>   it is being,

It is where expression should not mean,
An expedition in fear. ❏

Romaine Moreton, *a writer and performer, belongs to the nations of Bundjalung and Goernpil. © Romaine Moreton*

A sporting chance

'Whilst no one questions the place women occupy in the world of sport, the same is not true when it comes to their presence on governing bodies of clubs and federations. To this inequality we have to add inequalities relating to access to the sports themselves, to facilities, sponsorship, the actual conditions in which the sporting activity is carried out and the media attention paid to competitions and performance. As in any other area of society, the road that leads to recognition is much more difficult for women than for men. Moreover, for most women the weight of tradition and the division of labour in the family and in the home are major handicaps to their participation in outside activities and even more so to their taking on outside responsibilities.' *Marie-George Buffet, French minister for youth and sport*

ISABELLE AUTISSIER: ROUND-THE-WORLD SAILOR

'You have to be sure you're going to make it.

For a long time they used to say that a woman on board brought bad luck. They weren't even allowed aboard fishing boats. When I was a marine biologist and involved in experimental projects to measure fish, it was in my interests for them to get a good catch, and if they didn't, well, that was automatically my fault and they weren't slow to point it out! So, when it came to the round-the-world trip, I knew from the outset that, if it came to the choice between me, an unknown, and a boy who was an unknown as well, the skipper would instinctively go for the boy as a member of the racing team. That's why I decided straight away to go for single-handed sailing.

The public used to think only men could be involved in this sport

Brandi Chastain, celebrating the USA's victory in the Women's World Cup – Credit: Jed Jacobsohn/Allsport

because you needed strong arms. But most of the guys who win yacht races are not Rambos … In the 1960s and 70s, people used to say that it was a life for bums, unthinkable for a girl. It took girls like Florence Artaud or Catherine Chabaud to say: 'I don't give a damn, I'm going for it,' and to show that it's 95% a matter of intelligence. You don't have to make yourself super-fit, you'd be better off going and studying the weather forecasts. It's no harder for a woman than for a man: there are difficulties, sure, but they're the same ones.

I'm reasonably wise, I suppose, and I don't go looking for a punch-up! But I like tackling different problems or problems with a different slant. That's why I decided to stop doing the solo round-the-world race, because I've done it four times, and I'd certainly learn more by going in for the Volvo Race. You really have to be competitive for that one. It's not that I have a need to clobber the others, but I do have a need to push myself to the limits of what I can do.

The whole question of having a family is basic. Girls who do long-distance yacht races are all single and childless. All the boys of the same age who sail have children. There are definitely girls who decided not to go in for long-distance racing because they chose to have a family. When you're at sea you're not at home, and when you're on land you have an enormous amount of work to do.'

COLETTE BESSON: OLYMPIC ATHLETICS CHAMPION

'I want to get across to young people the pleasure to be found in sport.

I was lucky enough to be in the Mexico City Olympics and it was fantastic for a girl of 22 who was just breaking into top-level athletics to be selected, it was amazing … [But] Even when I won my Olympic title I didn't get as much media attention as the 4 x 100m men's relay, even though they only came third in the Olympics. I was Olympic champion, Olympic record holder and European record holder; it really was a bit much.

At the very top levels, training conditions are the same [for men and women]; the differences are in titles, in remuneration and in subsidies. They talk about equality between men and women but that will never happen in those areas … I think when I surprised everybody in 1968, I helped to demystify femininity a bit: here was a girl from the Charentes, running with her hair untied, not as muscle-bound as the others and beating everybody. She was able to break an Olympic record, become Olympic champion and still remain feminine. And the following year drove the point home even further when Nicole Duclos, who hadn't been in Mexico City, beat the world 400-metre record in Athens. Both of us helped women's sport by showing that you could run fast and still be a woman; in fact, Nicole was already the mother of a little girl at that stage.

[Today] women at the top level have the means to prepare themselves properly: once a woman shows she has real quality there will be a whole team around her making sure that she is working in the best possible conditions. Since she's going to be a source of income, they do everything they can to ensure success. Having said that though, Maurice Green and Marion John are two really good athletes, real quality, but he's always going to attract more media attention than she is. Even Marie-José Perec hasn't managed to change that, yet she's got an outstanding record of achievement.'

SANDRINE CHEIFFAUD: MEN'S RUGBY TRAINER AND MANAGER

'Training is a vocation, a challenge and a passion.

I can't say that I've been given much in the way of encouragement. They say that rugby is a sport where you come across a lot of macho men, but in fact they are the ones I have fewest problems with. They're quite quick to recognise your ability, your competence when it comes to directing a team. But there are others, the people you're going to upset. They're afraid you're going to take their jobs.

I suppose it's not *really* a very aesthetically attractive sport compared with others. It's quite hard to see a woman struggling or fighting. You do see women struggling but in other areas, not in a physical way, not involving physical contact. Boys don't see girls who play rugby as very attractive. There's a whole code of behaviour you have to adopt if you want to remain a girl and not a boy. There are some girls who get the two mixed up, and that's a pity.

Playing a boy's game is fine, but we're still girls. You don't behave like a man after a match; you're still a girl. It's not a matter of changing back into stiletto heels and a suit, but when it comes to how you behave and the 'post-match performance', you have to be careful if you want to be accepted in a milieu which is, after all, very masculine.

Since January [Sandrine Cheiffaud was appointed trainer to the Bressuire team in January 1999], I've met some really nice reporters; but there have been others who cover rugby who have made a few remarks. For a start, they were expecting someone quite burly and masculine, both in the way I spoke and in the way I behaved. I'm myself when I'm in trainers and shorts on the pitch, but afterwards you'll see me in jeans or, at other times, in a suit. Just because we play rugby we're not all masculine! I'm sorry that some of my fellow women players do behave in that way. They tend to drink a lot, to belch, and to be vulgar in their behaviour and their language. That's why we're not accepted in some areas; men are afraid of that sort of thing.

Some [reporters] were critical or sceptical. They said to themselves, is she as competent as they claim? Isn't it just a publicity stunt by the club and the Rugby Federation? Some of them stayed negative: they just can't accept seeing women in rugby at all. I'm not asking for their recognition; I don't have to prove anything to them. I've met people who claim to know the job [who] say I've only been let in at all because I was reasonably pretty.'

MICHELE MOUTON: WORLD RALLY CHAMPION RUNNER-UP

'For me a car has always meant freedom.

The titles I won in races where men and women are competing together mean more to me. I was runner-up World Champion in 1982, but you have to spell out that that title makes no distinction between men and women. I won four trials against all those men: San Remo in 1981, the Portuguese Rally in 1982, the Greek Rally and the Brazilian Rally, and I was the first and, at least up to the end of this century, the only woman to perform that feat.

I've no regrets and it has been a success story, but that doesn't mean that it's been easy. For example, in terms of mentality, because I only worked with men, I soon saw that, in the first trials, I was always one step behind because I needed to warm up, to get the feel of my car. I think that men and women react differently to these things. I always used to lose a precious few seconds at the beginning. In long-distance trials, on the other hand, over 100 kilometres in special trials, you reach your

Sandra Barnett, fastest-ever woman at the TT. The Isle of Man races are open, men and women competing side by side – Credit: Ian Kerr

own limits and those of the car too, and it's not easy to push a 500hp car to its limits and to keep doing that for 100 kilometres. There were moments when I said to myself: 'Do as they do, try not to think about it, don't worry about it, it'll do it or it won't.' Once you tell yourself that, you have to do it, you have to put your foot down and keep it there, no slowing down, no breaking.

It was a fantastic life; you really get to know yourself; you find out that you're capable of doing things that you'd never have dreamed you could. But now, no regrets.

[They] really annoyed me because, you know, at the end of a trial, whether it's 15 or 20 kilometres, you're sweating from head to foot. Even in Sweden, when it's minus 30 degrees outside, you're in a one-piece overall and you're soaked, because there's enormous nervous tension. So, every time there was a photographer there, they'd say: 'Smile, please!' I ended up hating that 'Smile, please!' and I always used to say: 'Do you ask Mikko or anybody else to smile? No, you just take him as he is.' But I always had to smile, I always had to look my best … that really got to me … Apart from that, I didn't have any serious problems … In fact, I couldn't have dreamed of anything better.'

Laila Ali's first pro fight, New York, 1999 – Credit: Al Bello / Allsport

YANNICK SOUVRE, CAPTAIN OF THE FRENCH BASKETBALL TEAM

'The Olympics is what I've always dreamed of.

Even supposing you get your expenses more or less paid, playing basketball at top level demands an enormous investment of time, so you don't have time for study. You have to make a choice but you don't get a salary to make up for it the way footballers or male basketball players might.

Very few girls get married. A few get engaged, but it's quite unusual because we have a vagabond's life. And in French society, it's still the woman who's expected to follow the man.

When it comes to drugs, the more money there is in sport, the more it risks being destroyed by drugs and backhanders. Women's basketball is small beer, but if there were three times as much money tomorrow, we might have to cope with the drugs problem. ❏

Edited excerpts from Le sport, elles en parlent *published by the feminist magazine* Lunes *in collaboration with the French ministry for youth and sport, Paris 2000. Translated by Nick Routledge*

GRANT FERRETT

Till the next time

On Saturday 24 and Sunday 25 June, Zimbabweans voted in the country's most fiercely fought parliamentary elections since independence in 1980. President Robert Mugabe's ruling party, ZANU-PF, was competing for a fifth term in office against the Movement for Democratic Change, which was formed last year. More than 30 people were killed in the three months before polling, nearly all of them opposition officials or sympathisers. In the majority of cases, the police failed to act. Three hundred foreign observers and thousands of local monitors watched the polling and the counting for signs of irregularities. As for international journalists: the place was swarming with them. This was the smart place to be...

SATURDAY 24 JUNE

Government-controlled daily newspaper, *Herald*, front-page lead story: 'ZANU-PF is headed for a landslide victory, shrugging off a token challenge from the white-backed opposition Movement for Democratic Change in this weekend's parliamentary elections, analysts said. The ruling party has been tipped to win for restoring peace, improving health and education facilities and because of its unwavering stance on land redistribution.'

Farmers' Hall Polling Station, Marondera East constituency
6:55am Presiding Officer, Thabani Ncube: 'Everything is fine. We will be opening for polling in five minutes. There are no problems.'

7:00am Independent Zimbabwean monitor, Penson Prasida: 'I'm very pleased to be here. I didn't think the government was going to allow us in. We didn't receive our accreditation until 8 o'clock last night. Then we had to drive here. Now we can watch what's going on. As you can see, there are already people queueing up to vote.'

7:20am Unidentified Voter: 'How did I vote? I'm afraid to tell you. There have been a lot of threats. Let's just say I voted for change.'

9:10am ZANU-PF candidate for Marondera East, Sydney Sekeramayi, minister of security: 'There has been no trouble here. The opposition has been allowed to campaign freely. It's just trying to disguise its lack of support. If I lose, I lose. There will be no violence.'

Polling Station, Highfield, Harare

10:30am Voter, Hopewell Mutisi: 'We queued for three hours. It was too long. They were very slow. But the people, they were happy. Some people gave MDC salutes [an open-handed wave], but the officials told them they must not do that near the polling station. We thought we would take off our shoes and wave with our feet instead.'

11:30am Pierre Schori, Head of European Union Observer Mission: 'I'm very happy with what I'm seeing here today. It's all going very peacefully and professionally. Also, when you see a lot of people queueing up to exercise their democratic right, that is very good. We will issue an interim report later.'

Aspindale School Polling Station, Mufakose, Harare

4:10pm Unnamed Independent Zimbabwean observers: 'We were allowed in the polling station for the first few hours, but then they told us to get out. Our accreditation was not issued last night. We were told to go and collect it too late. So we're staying outside. There are polling agents inside. They are watching. It would be better if we were inside.'

SUNDAY, 25 JUNE

Government-controlled *Sunday Mail*, front-page editorial: 'We are confident that Zimbabweans will vote for national sovereignty and that they will vote for land. As President Mugabe pointed out, this is an opportunity for Zimbabaweans to teach the British what democracy is all about.'

Sheraton International Hotel, Harare

10:30am Press Conference with John Nkomo, National Chairman of ZANU-PF: 'I have watched and listened with great concern the distortions and misrepresentations by the BBC, CNN, Sky TV and others. We wish to make it clear that media reports suggesting that these elections might lead to a change of government are more than wild. In terms of the constitution, ZANU-PF will most definitely form the next government, whatever the results of the legislative election.'

Polling Station, Stoddart Hall Polling Station, Mbare West, Harare

12:45pm Promise Chimisa: 'People have been crowding to ZANU-PF rallies because they didn't want to be killed. But what matters is what happens when you're in the polling booth, casting your vote. That's when the truth comes out. My vote is my voice.'

Meikles Hotel, Harare

3:30pm Press Conference with the leader of the MDC, Morgan Tsvangirai: 'The majority of Zimbabweans will be very disappointed if there's not an MDC victory. These elections are about real freedom from the corrupt, inept, arrogant leadership which has been running this country for the past two decades.'

Election Command Centre, Mukwati Building, Harare

6.30pm Press Conference with police commissioner, Augustine Chihuri: 'Now that the polls are about to close, it's important to let you know that we've deployed police to to try to maintain law and order. We appeal for the calm and peace of the voting period to be maintained. Reporter: 'Commissioner, will your officers enforce the law even-handedly after the results are announced?'
Chihuri: 'We will continue to uphold the law' (laughter).

Meikles Hotel, Harare

Midnight. Press Conference with Pierre Schori: 'The level of violence and intimidation in the pre-election phase makes the term "free and fair" not applicable to these elections.'

MONDAY 26 JUNE

Editorial in *Herald*: 'Zimbabwe has had a very bad international press in recent months. Those long patient queues of Zimbabweans determined to exercise their hard-won right to choose a new parliament will do much to neutralise the negative images, which had more to do with perceptions than reality.'

Allan Wilson School, counting centre for Harare Central Constituency
MDC candidate, Mike Auret: 'If they've fiddled it here, I'll want to know how. We've thought of every possible way and it seems not to have happened. It's gone very well over the weekend. If you see someone looking sullen, you know they're ZANU-PF.'

Election Command Centre, Mukwati Building, Harare
2pm Unnamed election official: 'Ladies and gentlemen. Our apologies for keeping you waiting. There is a delay. We will keep you informed.'

2.30pm Opposition supporters: 'We know why the results are late. They're doing what they always do – cheating. They're 'phoning Mugabe to ask what to do. They've lost and they're trying to rig it.'

4pm Reporter: 'The first results should have been announced five hours ago. What's the problem?
Registrar-general, Tobaiwa Mudede: 'Too many people voted.'

6.30pm Registrar-general, Tobaiwa Mudede, reads first result: 'Mpopoma Constituency, Bulawayo: MDC, 14,813. ZANU-PF, 2,540.

TUESDAY 27 JUNE

Privately-owned *Daily News*, front page: 'The ruling ZANU-PF yesterday had its first and worst electoral nightmare since coming to power in 1980. News of its defeat in constituencies in Harare sparked wild scenes of celebration in high-density areas which bore the brunt of politically-motivated violence in the run-up to the election. MDC supporters waved red cards and chanted slogans.'

Election Command Centre, Mukwati Building, Harare
1:45am Registrar-general, Tobaiwa Mudede, reads result for Marondera East Constituency: 'MDC, 10,629. ZANU-PF, 10,692.'

Mbare, Harare
10:30am Promise Chimisa: 'We won! We showed Mugabe we don't want him. We were out on the road singing and giving praise to ourselves. We didn't sleep until 4am. Before, some people were afraid, but now everyone here is showing their true colours.'

Meikles Hotel
11am Interview with Professor Jonathan Moyo, ZANU-PF Election Campaign Manager.
Reporter: 'Doesn't the fact that the opposition won nearly half the contested seats [Zanu-PF 62: MDC 57] mean President Mugabe has an obligation to give them half the 30 seats which he appoints?'
Moyo: 'There is no such legal obligation.'
Reporter: 'But isn't there a moral obligation?'
Moyo: 'Morality is always contested. Your morality is not necessarily my morality.'

Highfield, Harare
2pm Hopewell Mutisi: 'It was not enough. The people in the rural areas let us down. They were too scared. We are very disappointed. We can't wait two years for the elections for president. We will die before then.'

State House, Harare
8.30pm Televised address to the nation by President Mugabe: 'The majority [of the international observers and journalists] go away both humbled and educated, convinced and highly impressed how we do things here. How, against the background of a divisive and colonial legacy, we are all striving to overcome, we are still able to ensure that victorious and defeated are quick to reconcile, quick to connect and cohabit in the same national space for greater peace and togetherness. Well done, Zimbabweans! Keep it up!' ❏

Grant Ferrett *reports from Harare for the BBC*

upport for

NDEX

't is the generosity of our friends and supporters which makes *Index on Censorship's* work possible. *Index* remains the only international publication devoted to the romotion and protection of that basic yet still abused human right, freedom of xpression.

our support is needed more than ever now as *Index* and the Writers & Scholars ducational Trust continue to grow and develop new projects. Donations help directly wards such work as the expansion of our website, which will make access to *Index's* ories and communication between free-speech activists and supporters even easier, d the education programme, which will see *Index* fostering a better understanding f censorship and anti-censorship issues in schools.

ease help *Index* speak out.

he Trustees and Directors would like to thank the many individuals and organisations ho support *Index on Censorship* and Writers & Scholars Educational Trust, including:

If you would like more information about *Index on Censorship* or would like to support our work, please contact Hugo Grieve, Fundraising Manager, on (44) 20 7278 2313 or email hugo@indexoncensorship.org

Letter from Kigali

'The trouble is, the only people who really know about the genocide are all dead'

In the capital, Kigali, all is calm. As it is in the country as a whole. There's no evident army or police presence on the streets; there's no petrol shortage and the electricity supply has been restored. The shops are well stocked. Small building sites have sprung up all over the place and there are flowers in the flowerbeds. The hotels are charging top prices again and, only six years after the genocide, dollars can easily be had on the black market. Everything seems normal and there are no real signs of tension. A Belgian, who has just arrived even speaks of 'a haven of peace', although it's true he's only been here for three days and it's the first time he's set foot in Rwanda. Nevertheless, everyone agrees that peace has returned to Kigali. But at what price?

Finding out what's really going on in Rwanda is difficult and can be risky. If you stuck to the the golden rule of journalism – always use direct sources and get independent confirmation of the facts – most of the time you wouldn't be able to say a lot about anything at all. An untold number of Rwandan journalists, at one time close to the new leadership, have decided to leave the country; politicians have resigned and are making hasty exits to foreign parts; all in the face of death threats, serious or otherwise. Nothing can really be verified one way or the other. In the end, it all depends on whom you choose to believe.

Meanwhile, members of the Rwanda Patriotic Front, back from exile in Uganda, are quite obviously in the process of consolidating their hold on power and the media, accordingly, finds its freedom drastically curtailed. The transition period has just been extended to 2003, and General Kagame, the country's strongman since 1994, has just been elected by a parliament representing only the few parties that haven't been banned. He succeeded a president who had been accused of

'Pink shirt' genocide supects – Credit: Thierry Renavand/Sipa

corruption by his enemies and excess of political courage by others. The political parties have no right to free expression or assembly except abroad, where they are becoming increasingly numerous.

When I questioned a Rwandan official about the hasty departure of a local journalist who had just written an article judged highly critical, I was told that his article had been a deliberate provocation intended to obtain political asylum for him in some foreign country; as far as the Rwandan official was concerned, that was proof positive of conspiracy.

A Rwandan woman who has just returned after lengthy stays in the US and in France advises me: 'Never believe what a Rwandan tells you.' She was the one who looked me straight in the eye and told me: 'You only have to ask a Rwandan to eat grass or sand and he'll do it.' 'But that's why I'm here,' I told her, 'to hear what Rwandans have to say.' It scared her stiff.

A highly placed Rwandan tells me that the government has made no promises to the survivors and that they had to respond to the needs of all Rwandans. And then my informant went on to complain about the difficulty of getting any money out of the international community to help the survivors. On a later occasion, a volunteer who has been working in Rwanda for several years confirmed that donor countries are reluctant to put money into a fund set up for the survivors: the fund is entirely under the control of the government and appears to be strikingly lacking in transparency.

As far as the survivors themselves are concerned, the problem is far from straightforward. Officially – and it's a matter of political survival – they avoid any confrontation with the authorities; individually, they sometimes allow themselves to tell their tale of woe to a westerner, a *muzungu*. I asked why, and for once the answer was unambiguous: 'A *muzungu* can repeat what he likes to whomever he likes: no Rwandan will really believe him.' That's how one survivor came to tell me that the authorities often gave her the impression she was an embarrassment. 'I sometimes think they'd have preferred it if we'd all been massacred,' she muttered as we emerged from the town's stadium after a remembrance ceremony attended by a few officials and a scattering of people.

Listening to her, I thought about the testimony given by another woman a few weeks after the genocide: she had only survived because she had been left for dead among dozens of corpses lying on a classroom floor. I also remember the woman who was questioned in front of me and who confirmed that the Hutu militiamen who came to kill the Tutsis in her village had allowed her to choose between saving her son or her daughter and how she nodded when the interpreter told us that it was her son who was still alive. I remember asking whether she wanted the murderers found. She remained silent, but the interpreter told me that she knew them: they were her neighbours and they were in Zaïre. She said she wanted them tried but was prepared to forgive them because, she added, 'without forgiveness we could never manage to live together again'.

That was in 1994, and a few days later, I was in Zaïre with the hundreds of thousands of Rwandans fleeing the RPF. In the camps, I heard those who were authorised to speak claiming there had been no genocide, and I knew they were lying. When they assured me they had only lost the war temporarily and that they would return victorious, I knew that they were not joking and, during the two years that followed, I wouldn't have been surprised to see them do so. When they did suffer military defeat I had a sense of relief.

Since then, the Rwandans who fled, and who survived cholera, famine and the fighting, have been forced back home. The militiamen and the officers of the former Rwandan army who had trained them, and who had not been killed in the fighting, have enlisted as mercenaries in the armies facing each other in the Democratic Republic of Congo in what some are calling 'Africa's first world war'. Many of them are former enlisted men and have joined the new Rwandan army, dominated by the ruling RPF; they are now fighting their former leaders.

According to official figures, two million are supposed to have returned in 1996. I want to ask passers-by where they were in 1994; what they'd done; what their story was. Whenever possible, I do just that. People will talk to me about the war but never about the genocide. It is as if the word is simply not in their vocabulary. It isn't a matter of denying the genocide, but of not taking sides; and not one person I ask is prepared to say they spent even so much as a few months in Zaïre.

Not until I am invited to the house of a young woman whose family was completely wiped out during what she calls the 'war'; she escaped because she was in Burundi. She explains that she has come back to live in the house where her parents had been murdered and claims to get on well with the wives of her family's murderers. In fact, they work for her. Gradually, in answering my questions, they admit they fled to Zaïre and that their husbands fell ill and died in prison in Rwanda. 'Why don't you ask them what they think of the *gachachas*,' my hostess says. These are the traditional people's tribunals the government is thinking of setting up with the help of the international community. I see the fear in their faces, but what they actually say, with their heads bowed and their eyes on the ground, is: 'These are a good thing for finding out who has done something and who hasn't.'

Seeing them so poorly dressed and undernourished alongside their employer in the latest European fashion and her face well made-up, I leave with the feeling that they are the slaves of their protectress and that the voices of forgiveness are sometimes hard to understand.

A Belgian request for forgiveness is causing quite a stir, this time at the International Criminal Tribunal for Rwanda in Arusha, Tanzania, set up by the UN to try those implicated in the genocide. It comes from one Georges Ruggiu, who was active in broadcasting from Radio Mille Collines, the main voice of Hutu Power that night and day called on the Hutu population to exterminate the Tutsis, even directing them to the sites of action (see p105). After deciding to plead not guilty in 1997, Ruggiu finally changed his mind, pleaded guilty, agreed that what he had been involved in was indeed genocide and claimed he deeply regretted what had been done. He was sentenced to 12 years imprisonment; had he been tried in Rwanda, it could have been the death penalty. Indeed, like the 140,000 (in Rwanda, any number is an approximation which varies according to factors it is not always easy to establish) who are currently rotting in Rwandan prisons, he might even have been denied a trial for years – unless he had confessed and so jumped the queue.

I made a brief visit to a prison in 1994 and it seemed like a picture of hell; I'd been afraid. Six years later, the situation is still the same in some jails but, if you have the means to pay, you can do all right: you can get yourself a pink uniform, something you have to have to get a job in a workshop, in particular, the workshops which make pink uniforms. Or you can get a job on one of the weeding teams outside the prison: the detainees have no handcuffs or shackles and there are few guards; it's as if they had been placed in the custody of the population as a whole.

Prisoners are sentenced to death and publicly executed regularly in the hope of preventing history in Rwanda from repeating itself. I have not been present at an execution, but I do remember what I saw in a detention camp for children. Some of them were proud of themselves and respected because they had killed more people than the others, a claim they were happy to confirm with a broad grin. But when I asked them why, they would say nothing. I remember how their big, dark eyes gleamed and how I couldn't hold their gaze. There were about 40 boys with a teacher who could only work with them one day a week because of lack of funds. They had been shut away so that they wouldn't be lynched by the relatives of those they'd murdered. Simultaneously, in the same country, other boys, scarcely any older than they, are being recruited into the army after being trained at military camps specially set up for them. ❏

From an Index *correspondent*